MIKE deM

Five Year Vest

Why

I Quit

The NYC

Police

Department

MIKE deMARINO

ISBN: 1-59232-201-8

Seaburn Books
P.O. Box 2085
Long Island City, NY 11102

Seaburn offers quantity discounts to institutions and to
bookstores. Volume discounts are also available for schools
and for fundraising events.
For more information, visit www.seaburnbooks.com

Cover designed by Andreas

Printed in the United States of America

2

Five Year Vest

MIKE deMARINO

The time is about 1:00 A.M. on a weeknight. It's a nice, quiet night on patrol in the South Bronx. My partner is driving the patrol car at a snail's pace the wrong way down a one way street, staying as close as he can to the parked cars. This is an easy way to see the expiration dates on the inspection and registration stickers on the windshields. I'm sitting in the passenger's seat, half asleep, enjoying the calmness of the night. The only thought that I entertain is wondering when the central dispatcher will bother us with a job. But this time it's not going to be "central" calling us.

"We have a foot pursuit central, we need backup!" The officer's voice ripped through the silence of the night. "Unit, what's your location?" central demanded. My partner and I are staring at our radios impatiently waiting for the response. "Central, we're at …" The officer can hardly get the words out. "We're at 143 Street and Willis Avenue!" My partner and I are just around the corner and up the block. As my partner puts the car in reverse, I tell "central" that we are backing up that unit. It felt like we were going ninety M.P.H. down the block in reverse when I felt the car start to swerve. Out of the corner of my eye I can see my partner struggling to control the car, when a split second later my head is jerked from the impact as we slam into two parked cars. My partner and I look at each other with an "oh shit" expression on our faces. I scream to my partner "Fuck it, let's go. We'll deal with this later!" As we turn the corner and race down the block, we pass the pursuing officer and catch up to the fleeing suspect. As my partner slows the car down to keep pace with the Perp, I pull on the door handle and get prepared to jump out and tackle him when I notice that he is keeping

4

his right hand in the waist line of his pants. The first thought that enters my mind is that he has a gun. I don't want to get shot, so I hesitate. Suddenly, the Perp stops in front of an empty lot and starts to climb the chain link fence that encircles it. Now I can see that there is no gun so I jump out of the car and run to grab the Perp before he makes it over. The officer that was pursuing the Perp on foot reaches the fence at the same time I do. The Perp makes it over, just barely avoiding our grasp. As I look through the fence into the darkness to see if I can catch a glimpse of the suspect, I hear a thud. I look to my right and see the officer that was in the foot pursuit laying flat on his back. I hear my partner say "Oh shit, Frankie!" as I drop to my knees along side the downed officer. When I look at Frankie's face, I see his eyes roll up into his head and his mouth drop wide open. "Breathe Frankie, Breathe!" I scream, but all he can do is gag. I start engaging CPR as the other officers approach. I hear my sergeant cry out "I think he's been shot!" "He's not shot; he's having a fucking heart attack!" I yelled. As I hear a call for the ambulance come over the radio, my partner races our patrol car as close to me as he can without killing me, and we proceed to lift Frank off the sidewalk and into the backseat of the patrol car. My partner and another officer race off to the hospital and I'm left standing there watching, and praying. My hands are covered in Frank's blood that was rushing out of the gash in the back of his head that resulted when he collapsed and struck his skull on the pavement. When everything slowed down and I was able to collect myself mentally, I told the sergeant on the scene what had transpired. I mentioned the slight car accident that we had on the other block. That's no big deal. All we had to do was complete the proper paper work and that will be straightened out.

I could only imagine what the scene at the emergency room was like. I finally got a ride to the hospital where I was met by my partner. "The doctor had to zap Frankie twice with the paddles, but he's going to be okay." Hearing my partner again was a relief that no words can describe. My partner and I were told by the doctor that if we would have waited for the ambulance Frank would've never made it and that the CPR probably saved his life. So my partner and I are heroes. That's really not important. Frankie is alive. We did our job. Besides, a hero is nothing but a sandwich.

CHAPTER 1

Whenever anybody would ask, "Hey Mike, what's the NYC Police Academy like?" I always gave the same answer: high school. There was cheating on tests, cutting class, and falling asleep in class. In high school, this is expected from some students. But in the police academy, one would expect a much more disciplined atmosphere. That's what I thought. The only real difference is that in high school there is the possibility of failing. But to fail out of the academy you would literally have to have an empty space between your ears. Even if you had a head full of shit, they would find a way to pass you. Of course I didn't know this when I took the entrance exam. I mean this is the N.Y.P.D. - serious stuff-.

Throughout my three years in high school I did my fair share of sleeping, cutting, and cheating. Don't get me wrong, I'm a fairly bright guy. But, I'm also lazy. On top of that, I hated school. I would only do the minimum necessary to pass. I really didn't know what I wanted to do career wise so my father suggested that I take the police test. I never in my wildest dreams ever considered being a cop, but it takes about a year to be called by the department after taking the test, and who knows what I'll be doing at the time I am called. I could always turn the job down. So I followed my old man's advice and signed up for the entrance exam.

The entrance exam is what I like to call an idiot's test. You have to be an idiot to fail it. The day I took the test I was still awake and drunk from the night before. The test was given at my old high school. Thinking back to the three years that I spent in this school, I'm finally taking a test that meant something in my life. I probably should've stayed home the night before and got a good night's sleep, but old habits are hard to break.

I sat down at my desk and tried to pay some attention to the instructions being given by the proctor. The tests were distributed along with the personal information sheets. I sat there and painfully followed the slow, deliberate instructions from the proctor. Because we all know how hard it is to read, "Last name, First name" and not know what to do. I'm being sarcastic, but I can't help it. Anyway, everybody finished filling out the necessary information and the test began.

The exam consisted of a hundred multiple-choice questions in which you have four hours to finish. When I started to read the first few questions, I couldn't believe how easy this was. Ninety-five percent of the test is reading comprehension. If you know how to read, then you should pass the test. After I answered the hundredth question, I double and triple checked my answers. When I looked at the time, I was surprised to see that only an hour and a half had passed. I was sure that I messed up somehow. Maybe I skipped a bunch of questions. I should check my answers again. BUT, with every minute that passed, the more sober I got, and the more hung over I became. I handed in my test, went home and passed out.

The next day, I went to work and continued my life as a telemarketer selling industrial cleaning chemicals to unsuspecting fools. Volunteer fire departments, waste treatment plants and catholic churches paid my bills for the next year. But telemarketing is tough, mentally exhausting. I've had several jobs in my life but this was the first one that would knock me out mentally. When I was eighteen, I worked for the teamsters at the Nassau Coliseum unloading trucks for concerts. That was hard work, physically draining. But after work, I could still go to the bar for a beer, or go out to dinner with my girlfriend.

But after spending eight hours in an office trying to make phone sales, all I wanted to do after work is go home and veg out. If I had to choose between physical exhaustion and mental exhaustion, I would take the physical kind every time. I was doing the phone sales for about three years before I took the police test. But in the fourth year, I started to get burned out. I would make an average of about eighty calls a day, some days without one sale. The last thing that I wanted to look at when I got home was a telephone. Some days when I was really stressed out, I would think back to my very first job working in a pet store. That was the best job I ever had. Since I'm a reptile lover, it was perfect. The store was owned by a couple of guys who were left over hippies from the sixties. Working for two guys who were just as laid back as I was, resulted in a stress level of zero. Being fifteen with no real responsibilities didn't hurt either. I worked at the pet store off and on for seven years. I quit for a while to do the teamster job that I mentioned earlier. I would've kept the teamster job, but I tore up my knee playing football and couldn't consistently do the heavy lifting that the job required so I went back to the good old pet store.

From the age of fifteen up until the telemarketing job, I bounced around with different jobs starting with the pet store, to movie usher, pizza deliveryman, and teamster. As long as I had some sort of income, I was happy. What was more important to me, as well as more enjoyable, was hanging out with my friends. The one thing that I feel really lucky about is that I have kept the same close group of about fifteen friends since grade school. I don't know how many people can say that. My friends and I did things like play stickball, see concerts, kayak down the Delaware River and go fishing.

As we were growing up, going through our teenage years, and our twenties, we always managed to keep life simple. As long as we could get together, either it was hanging in the park with some beer or going to a bar, we were happy. We never really got into trouble. All we wanted to do was hang out and enjoy ourselves.

As I said earlier, I was in the fourth year with the phone sales and I needed a change. I'm a twenty-five year old man, and I felt that I was at an age where I can't just quit and start bouncing around from job to job again. Also, I was dating a woman that worked in the sales office and our relationship was starting to get serious. I really liked Raquel, and I didn't want her to think she got involved with a bum.

I remember her first day walking into the office. She entered through the office door and had a confident, yet snobbish look on her face as she strutted passed me and the other salesmen to the manager's office. She was wearing a business suit that had no business fitting her the way it did. I figured that a woman like this has to have a boyfriend, or fiancée or something. But as time went by, we would go for drinks after work and got to know each other, I started to feel a little chemistry between us. I finally got the courage to ask Raquel on a date and she gladly accepted. On a Saturday morning at 6:00 AM, I was standing on line at Madison Square Garden to buy a pair of tickets to the Ringling Bros. Circus. We went for dinner and had a great time. I was the envy of all the guys at the office. Raquel and I were married five years later and I couldn't be happier.

Raquel ended up becoming the top salesperson at the office. She has a real knack for it. I, on the other hand, am no salesman. The only reason that I was able to do the job and be somewhat successful at it is because I'm a personable guy with a halfway decent head on my shoulders. I needed to find a profession that I could stay with into my retirement. I thought about going back to school, but school didn't work the first time around so I doubt that it would be any different a second time. Every day I checked the want ads to see what I could find, and every day I found the same thing; nothing.

11

CHAPTER 2

Then, one fateful day, in my mail, there it was. It was the letter that stated that I had passed the entrance exam and must complete the enclosed form to start the character investigation for the police academy. I completed the form as fast as I could, totally aceing the first name, last name stuff, and mailed it. My journey to be a N.Y.C. Police Officer has officially started. How hard could the job be? My father was a cop in the sixties, but he rolled over to the fire department after only six years on the job, a popular move by a lot of cops. My sister has been a cop for fifteen years now and she used to pop popcorn at the movie theater before that, and her husband is a sergeant with sixteen years on. If you ever met my family, you would think that I could be promoted all the way to commissioner!

After a week or so since I mailed in the form, I receive a phone call. "Hello?" "Hello, can I please speak to Mr. DeMarino?" The Jamaican accent is so strong that I can hardly understand him. "Yeah, this is him." I replied with a bit of uncertainty. "Mr. DeMarino, this is Investigator Jones. I need to see you to start your investigation for the Police Academy." His accent has me convinced that this is a friend of mine playing a joke on me. "Very funny," I said. "Keith, is that you". My friend Keith has a history of making prank calls to his friends. After my accusation, there is a short moment of silence. "Mr. DeMarino, this is ...." He repeated himself. Oops, my mistake. We got passed the semi embarrassing moment and scheduled my first meeting.

I showed up at the investigator's office looking quite presentable. Shirt and tie, slacks, shoes, I mean the whole nine yards.

"How are you Mr. DeMarino?" His accent is a little more tolerable in person. "The first thing you have to do is cut your hair." I thought that I had misunderstood him due to his accent. "Excuse me?" I said. "You are not allowed to have long hair on the police department." I understood that perfectly. I couldn't believe it. I had long hair since I'm sixteen. I could never picture myself with short hair. When Samson cut his hair, it ruined him. But, if that's the rule then so be it. After all, this is the N.Y.P.D. Time to grow up. "No problem" I said. "It will be cut tomorrow." Meanwhile, I'm thinking to myself how glad I am that I removed my tongue ring before the interview. I'll get back to the tongue ring later on.

"Mr. DeMarino, I need you to take these forms home, complete them, and bring them back on your next visit." Okay, so I have to fill out some forms. No big deal. I never was more wrong. The investigator started to pull forms out of every drawer, and file on his desk. When he was finished, I walked out of his office shell-shocked. I was holding a stack of forms in my arms that I couldn't believe. There were forms requiring proof of residence, proof of employment, proof of education, proof you're a human living on earth, etc. What am I going to do? I can't fill all this stuff out. I don't have the patience. I needed help, professional help, and I needed it fast.

"Mom! I'm home and I have to fill out these forms." Need I say more? Every son should have a mom like mine. I'm not just saying that because she's my mom, well, I am but I really mean it. Remember that I worked in a pet store during my youth. Every few weeks I would come home with a different animal. At one point, I had fifteen different creatures in my room. Everything, ranging from scorpions to lizards. I even had a four foot Caiman alligator for a while. But, snakes were my favorite. To this day I still have my king snake that I bought back in 1988. Needless to say, I pushed both my parents patience to its limit. My father was a lot less understanding than my mom was, so my mom and I lived by one simple rule: Don't tell dad.

I sure as hell didn't tell my dad when my python escaped and was lost somewhere in the house. I figured that I would find it eventually. How many places can a six foot snake hide? Of course, as fate would have it, my old man was the one to find the snake. We had a big, old television set in the den that didn't work. My father decides one day to try to fix it. When he unscrewed the back panel, I heard him scream my name in a way that I knew I was in trouble for something. The last thing my father expected to see inside a television is a snake. "Oh, good. You found my snake." I said very innocently as I walked into the den. "Found your snake?! I didn't even know the god damned thing was missing!" My father's face was bright red. He was probably more surprised than angry. The

14

snake had been missing for a total of two months until my father found it. I assumed that it should be hungry. I bought two mice from the pet store, but the snake wouldn't eat. I put the mice in a bucket and covered it with the yellow pages. I figured I would try to feed the snake again tomorrow. The only problem is that we have two cats in the house. Cats are not stupid. They can smell the mice in the bucket and proceed to knock the bucket over.

Now there are two mice loose in the house and the cats are going nuts. I let my mom in on the situation, and she says, "Don't tell your father." I told her that the cats will eventually catch them anyway and dad will never know. But, once again, fate would have its fun with me. My father decides to go to bed early, and a few minutes after he closes his bedroom door, I hear him screaming my name and cursing. He comes running out of the bedroom, wearing only his underwear. "There's two god damned mice in my bed!" There are plenty of places for a mouse to hide in my house. There is the upstairs, the basement, and three other rooms on the main floor, but these mice have to hide in my father's bed, under the covers with him, and start to crawl on his legs, scaring the shit out of him.

These are just two instances out of dozens that I have put my parents through. Not all involved animals. I once accidentally set the house on fire and also caused a flood. Not all at the same time, but I'm not going to go into details. Of course whenever one of my "instances" occurred, my father would say to my mother, "That's YOUR son, you know."
So having me come home with a stack of forms that I needed help filling out was a walk in the park for my mother.

CHAPTER 3

I showed up at the investigator's office a few days later with the completed stack of forms that "I" slaved over. "Mr. DeMarino, I need you to complete one more form". My investigator hands me a form consisting of three questions. Question 1: Do you have any tattoos? Question 2: If yes, How many? And Question 3: What do they mean to you? I looked over the questions and wrote down my answers in the shortest form possible. 1: Yes. 2: three. 3: They mean nothing to me. What kind of answer does the department expect me to write down? That the voices in my head told me to get tattoos? As far as my tattoos are concerned, I just like the artwork. I don't have any giant swastikas, or satanic images, or things of that nature tattooed on me. But, I guess the police department wants to try to weed out any possible racists, or other unwanted types as early as they can. I love my tattoos and that's all that matters.

By now you should have a mental picture of me. Long hair, tattoos and a tongue ring. If you ever saw me you would think that the last thing I would be is a cop. But, when you do the minimum throughout school just to skate by, you end up not being qualified to do much else. Believe me when I say that I hated school, but if I had the chance to do it all over again, I would be a much different student. But, as the saying goes, "Hind sight is 20/20."

A few weeks into the character investigation, the time came for the written psychological exam and interview. The written exam was about fifteen hundred multiple-choice questions. I'm not kidding. The test is designed to see if there is any consistency to your answers. For example, questions five, four hundred, and eleven hundred can be the same questions, only they are worded differently. When the tests are "graded," and they see that you didn't answer these questions the same, I guess that tells them something about your mental health. As far as I'm concerned, answering fifteen hundred questions gets very monotonous. After answering about seven hundred questions, my heart just isn't into it anymore. I start reading the questions half fast, skimming through them to finish the damn test. Whatever conclusion they determine about me can't be that accurate. Besides, after answering so many questions, I felt like I started to lose my mind.

A week or so later, it was time for the psychological interview. One on one with a shrink, who will ask me questions, based on the test results, and in this one meeting will determine if I am mentally qualified to be a police officer.

My sister and her husband told me to be very careful during the interview. They told me that the interview can last for hours, and that the shrink will try to trick you. They did a good job making me nervous, but I was ready for the challenge. "Just tell them what they want to hear." That was the last piece of advice that my sister gave me. The idea is to tell the truth, but curb it if you have to.

17

I couldn't have been any luckier than I was on the day of my interview. One of the shrinks called in sick at the last minute. Now they were short handed for the day and had to do a complete rush job. My interview lasted all of fifteen minutes. When I walked into the psychologist's office, I expected to see an old man with a long, messy beard. Instead, I was greeted by a very harmless looking older woman. She reminded me of my grandmother. "Come in and sit down Mr. DeMarino." She looked at me and smiled. She seemed nice enough I thought, but I kept my guard up. "How are you today?" she asked. "I'm fine," I answered. I paused and looked around her office and with a smile on my face, I asked "I thought I was going to be laying on a couch for this." As she laughed, I was hoping that I had lightened the mood a little.

She proceeded with the interview and asked basic, simple questions. "Are you close to your parents?" "Do you get along well with others?" Things of that nature. I heeded my sister's advice and gave the obvious answers. "Do you drink," she asked with a look on her face that told me she was especially interested in this one. "Well, I might have a toast on New Year's Eve." I told the truth, but I didn't leave myself open for follow up questions. The last question that she asked me was "Why did you want to be a police officer?" "Because I was a fuck up in school, and I need a real job". I didn't say that, but when I think back, I wonder what her reaction would have been if I did give that answer. "Because I want to help people" was the reply that I offered. That question was what I like to refer to as a ground ball, or a piece of cake. Interview over.

I didn't realize just how easy I got off with my interview until I bumped into my friend Chris a few days later in the city. We became friends back in high school but lost touch with each after we graduated. "Hey Chris, how ya been?" I asked as I extended my right hand to greet him. "Pretty good, man. Long time, no see." He replied as he shook my hand and we patted each other on the back. After we exchanged pleasantries and joked about our high school days, he told me that he was in the process of becoming a cop. When I told him the same, neither one of us could believe it. He told me that he went through the psychological interview yesterday and I asked him how it went.

I could tell by the tone in his voice that he was still frustrated by the whole experience. Chris went on to explain that the first question the psychiatrist asked him was "How often do you get angry?" "I really don't get angry." Chris replied. Chris then said that the shrink leaned forward in his chair and looked Chris dead in the face and said, "You mean to tell me that you NEVER get mad! Well, then we are going to sit here until you get angry." The psychiatrist then crossed his arms, put his feet up on the desk, and leaned back in his chair. The two of them sat there staring at each other. "Mike, I sat there for almost forty minutes with the asshole staring at me waiting for me to react. We didn't say one word to each other the whole time. Finally, the shrink moved on with the questioning."

I'm sure that Freud would be proud. Chris and I both passed the psychological part. So far, so good.

CHAPTER 4

About a week later, I received a letter informing me about the pre-medical and drug test. I wasn't really concerned about the pre-medical test. I'm very active in sports and kept myself in o.k. shape. The pre-med test consists of measuring your height, weight, and body fat. If your weight doesn't coincide with your height, then you are told what the ballpark weight you should be and you are scheduled for a retest at a later date. The same goes for your body fat. Also, you are required to fill out a medical history form detailing all injuries and/or surgeries you had while growing up. I've had my share of both. I played organized football with the Pop Warner league for eight years and suffered through a broken left wrist, elbow surgery, and reconstructive knee surgery, not to mention the countless ligament sprains and concussions.

As I was filling out the pedigree info on the form, I thought to myself, what if I didn't tell them anything? How would they know? I couldn't imagine that the department can check every candidate's medical history file, so why open up a possible can of worms. For all I know, the department might send me to be reevaluated by one of their doctors just to make sure that I'm medically capable or something. We were instructed that if we never had any injuries or surgeries to write down 'Nothing to report'. That made sense to me. I took a peek at the guy sitting next to me to see what he had listed and let me tell you, he had a pretty impressive list. The one thing that this guy wrote that stood out was 'shot in left foot'. I thought that was a little too much info to give the P.D., so I wrote, with hesitation, 'nothing to report'. The forms were collected and we were led in groups of about fifteen into an examination room where a doctor would examine us based on the information we wrote down. The doctor instructed us to strip down to our underwear and when your name is called, to come and stand in front of his desk. The doctor called us one by one to stand in front of us while he read our 'injury report' and looked us over. Now I'm thinking that I'm busted. I was sure that he was going to see my surgical scars and ask me why I lied on the form. "DeMarino, you're next!" I slowly walked over to his desk with my head down. As I stood there, he read over my form, looked up at me and asked, "You're fine?" "I'm fine." I answered him back very quickly. "Okay". He said. "Get dressed." That was it. That was the extent of the physical examination.

I said that I wasn't worried at all about the pre-med test. But, the drug test was another story. I'm not implying that I'm a drug addict, but I never did take Nancy Reagan's advice and just said no. I wasn't' worried about it until I received the notification for the drug test in the mail. The test date is in seven days!

This was not enough time to be ready for a drug test. I needed a least a month to make sure that my system was clean. What made matters worse was the fact that it was not going to be a

21

urine test. There are ways to beat a urine test. Drinking that special tea, for example. But this was going to be a hair test. I was told that with a hair test, they can check back as far as five years. I'm doomed. All those summer nights hanging out with friends, enjoying a joint was going to catch up with me.

After they cut off a lock of my hair and sent it to be examined, I would check my mail every day, with hesitation, and the fear of receiving a termination letter.

All I kept thinking about was all the time I had wasted with the investigation up until now. The worse part would be telling my family that I failed the drug test. Well, I obviously passed. I don't know how, nor do I care.

I finished the rest of the investigation process without a problem.

CHAPTER 5

The big day had finally arrived - Orientation at Queens College. It was the middle of July and it was hot. We had to wear proper business attire. As soon as I arrived, I had to fall into line and stand at attention. We had to stand there until just about everybody showed up. We stood like this for over an hour in the hot sun sweating like pigs. I guess the discipline had officially started.

When we were finally led into the auditorium, we were seated in groups of about thirty-five people. This group was going to be my official company and classmates for the next eight months.

Several speakers representing the academy took turns addressing us. Sergeants, lieutenants, captains and above took turns informing us what was to be expected of us during our training. The one point that all the speakers seemed to stress was that the police department is a para military organization and discipline is a must. I was never in the military so hearing this made me nervous. The closest I came to being in the military is after high school, I told my dad that I didn't want to go to college. My dad responded with four words, "College or the army." I chose college. As it turns out, this made a lot of us nervous because about ten people quit at the end of the first day of orientation! I don't know how someone could quit based on only what they were being told. The sad part is that after about a month into the academy, I realized that all this para military talk was bullshit. It is an insult to our armed forces that this would be considered even a fraction of what our military is all about. Like I said, I was never in the military but if our military is similar to this, then our country is in big trouble. The only thing the academy does that is similar to the military is marching to a cadence. That's about it. Oh yeah, and saluting.

As the speakers continued to take their turns on stage, this one female sergeant approached the podium with a seriously bad ass look on her face like she was the devil himself, or herself in this case. When she started to speak, it seemed as if she was looking at each and every one of us one at a time. Her head slowly turned from side to side and her eyes didn't seem to blink. She spoke in a strong, monotone voice like a robot. She started to address us on proper personal appearance in the academy. "Men, your hair must be closely shaved and follow the general shape of your head" she commanded as fire shot from her eyes. "And the women must keep your hair up and off your shirt collars. Also, there will be no jewelry allowed. Any questions?" Here's were my tongue ring comes back into the picture. I raised my hand, stood up, and said, "Excuse me, ma'am." We were instructed to start all questions in this manner, unless of course it's a man speaking, in which case you would say 'excuse me sir'. Anyway, I stood up and said "Excuse me, ma'am, but what about non visible body piercing?"

With that one question I managed to turn that cold, hard look on her face into a look of confusion as the entire class of sixteen hundred recruits proceeded to give me a roaring ovation. "Non visible body piercing," she asked. "I don't want to know where it is as long as I can't see it." To this day, I swear that she answered me with a hint of a smile on her face. Throughout my five years on the job, cops that were in my academy class would come up to me and shake my hand telling me how much they enjoyed my question. If I'm going to be remembered for something, why not this?

In the academy, we will be taught in three academic courses. They were Police Science, Law, and Social Science. The classes taught by cops, who, for one reason or another, have been assigned to the academy to be instructors. Police Science is the studying of the patrol guide. This is the rule book that governs a cop's responsibility, and proper way of handling a situation. The Law is the study of the law. That's pretty obvious. But, I guess it is pretty important for a cop to not only know when someone is breaking the law, but also which law is being broken. And Social Science is to teach us how to talk to people and use what the department calls 'verbal judo' to defuse a situation without using physical force. This can be quite effective except that the only 'verbal judo' that most cops use is "Get against the fucking wall or else I'll break your face!"

Throughout our learning we will be given four quarterly exams based on the three courses and must maintain an average score of seventy to graduate. The other class is the physical education class. In this class, we are supposed to be taught self-defense, proper tactics, and CPR. Now, I used the word 'supposed' because what they actually "teach" us is a form of show and tell.

25

MIKE deMARINO

First they show us, and then they tell us that we're ready for the street. It's a shame how unprepared cops really are for the street when they graduate. If there was ever a contest where they placed a newborn baby in the middle of the Amazon Rain Forest and at the same time released a new, academy trained cop into Harlem, my money is on the baby surviving longer. There are cops who have "street smarts", but "street smarts" is not something that can be taught. That's why it's called "street smarts". People who grew up with this quality are automatically, better suited to be cops.

One would be inclined to believe that the cops assigned to the academy to teach us are or were real go getters that should pass their superior knowledge of policing on to us. Well, think again. Most of the cops teaching in the academy were either jammed up, that's police jargon for getting in trouble with the job, and were sent to the academy as punishment, or couldn't handle the stress of being on patrol and needed a break. For example, one of the gym instructors left her gun in the bathroom at a bar and she got 'jammed up' and was banished to the academy. My Police Science instructor had a nervous breakdown on patrol and was reassigned to the academy for a break. What's even more mind boggling is the fact that he told us he failed the sergeants exam, which is based on the patrol guide, and now he's teaching Police Science. If an electrician is showing you how to wire a switch, you wouldn't expect him to get electrocuted. He should know what he's talking about. Do you get my point?

There are some cops in the academy that requested to be there so they can get better prepared for an up coming promotional

26

exam. Then there are those that know someone in a high ranking position on the force and would ask them to pull strings at police headquarters and have that cop placed in the academy or pretty much any other detail the cop wanted. That's called having a "hook." The more powerful your "hook," the more options you will have available to you. One reason why a cop would choose to be transferred to the academy besides for studying purposes is that the cop is lazy and doesn't want to do police work anymore. And at the academy, you are a cop without being a cop. You're a teacher with a badge. Plain and simple.

The academy class consisted of approximately sixteen hundred recruits that were split into two squads, A and B. We would have class five days a week with weekends off. The two squads would alternate between working morning hours and afternoon hours every week. The morning hours were from 8:00 A.M. to 4:00 P.M., while the afternoon hours are from 4:00 P.M. to midnight. So, one week squad A is scheduled to work the day tour, and squad B would work the afternoon tour. The following week it would be the opposite, and so on.

Each squad consisted of about thirty-five companies and each company was comprised of about thirty-two to thirty-five recruits. The group of recruits that I was seated with at the orientation were going to be my official company. We were company #8. We were told to all meet at the designated uniform store to buy our academy uniform. After we all arrived, we were greeted by our official company instructor, Officer Paul. The official company instructor was equivalent to a high school homeroom teacher. He was the one responsible for us. If we had any problems or needed help, we would go to him first. P.O. Paul was also our Law instructor. He was one of the few cops that asked to be in the academy so he could prepare for the next sergeant exam. A year or so after I graduated, I heard that he passed the test and was working in Brooklyn as a sergeant. Good for him. He was a really nice guy.

If we were told once, we were told a million times that the Police Department is a para military organization and that discipline is a must. Each recruit was issued a number of index cards that were called demerit cards. Whenever a recruit would screw up, they would loose one demerit card. This would include being late, having a messy uniform, not shaving, etc. If you loose seven cards, then you will be issued what's called a Command Discipline which can result in a loss of vacation days as punishment. C.D.'s are used to punish cops on the street as well. But, cops on the street can also get in trouble for things like not showing up to court when needed, not filling out the proper paperwork or just pissing off a supervisor. Depending on the severity of the C.D., a cop can lose anywhere from one hour of vacation time to ten days or more. I worked with this one cop that had lost thirty days of vacation time in one shot. That's a whole year's worth.

The 'crime' that this particular cop committed was that he got a second job without getting authorization from the Department. There are department forms that you need to fill out detailing what the off duty job will consist of. The department will then determine if they will allow you to work at that particular job. This is because the department feels the need to control every aspect of your life, on and off duty. Also, the department doesn't want cops to abuse their power and the fact that they have a gun working at certain security jobs. The department is worried about its public image. The last thing it needs is an off duty cop shooting or hurting someone at a club that the cop is bouncing at and the next thing you know it's all over the morning papers.

So this one cop that I know got himself a part time job working the door at a club somewhere in upstate New York. He probably figured that no one would find out. Well, another cop must have seen him working there and ratted him out to a supervisor, because one day he was busted and the outcome was the loss of thirty vacation days. I think I would have quit on the spot if I lost that many days.

During my eight months in the academy, I lost four cards. Not bad. To my surprise, I found the classes more interesting that I thought I would. In law, I found that the law is structured to protect the rights of the criminal. There are so many particulars that go into arresting someone that I would say about ninety percent of arrests that are made are not done completely legal. But, then again, if it were made easier for cops, there would be a lot more cops on the worse power trip than they already are.

In Police Science, all you have to do is know the patrol guide and learn what your responsibilities are in any given situation. The one problem with this is that on the street there is a lot of improvising, and split second decisions being made. You can't always do something the way the patrol guide dictates. The favorite thing that a supervisor will say when examining the way a cop handled something is to say "Does it say to do that in the patrol guide?" My favorite response to that is "Sir, It's called a patrol GUIDE, not a patrol bible." When a cop gets promoted and doesn't do patrol anymore, they seem to forget what it's all about. Also, most cops let the new found authority go to their head and they become real pricks and forget that we are all in this together.

The Social Science class was really just common sense. I consider myself to be a fairly nice guy that knows how to talk to people with respect. That's pretty much what this class is all about.

The gym class was the worst. For the men it was a miserable experience while the girls had it easy. Let me explain. There are approximately six companies in the same gym class at once. Since there are only an average of four girls in each company, that adds up to about twenty-five to thirty girls in the gym. Compare that to an average of a hundred and eighty guys, I think you can imagine the difference between the two locker rooms. Believe me when I say that I have seen enough naked men in that locker room, that if I live to be a thousand years old and never see another naked man again, I'll die happy. The men's locker room was so disgustingly crowded that one day the girls complained of having mice in their locker room, the running joke was that there wasn't enough room in the men's locker room for mice!

Every gym class started out with us standing at attention and saluting the flag. Then we started in with the calisthenics that included jumping jacks, sit ups, push ups, etc. After the calls came the run. Everybody dreaded the run. We would run at least twenty-five laps around the gym led by one of the instructors. The number of laps depended on the instructor. There were some instructors that only ran the twenty-five laps, but others would make us run forty, fifty, even ninety laps. With over two hundred people running in a small gym, it gets like an oven. After a few weeks, we would learn which instructors were the ones that liked to run and which ones didn't. We were told that if you can't complete the run, to fall out. But, we were warned that if we drop out of the run before completing the mandatory twenty-five laps, it will be documented, and if you drop out an 'x' amount of times, then you may not graduate. This turned out to be a crock of shit as most of the training would turn out to be. The same people would drop out every day before the first twenty-five laps, but were standing there with me on graduation day getting sworn in by the mayor at Madison Square Garden.

After the run, we would be sent back to our lockers to grab our police gear and start learning self-defense, proper tactics and techniques. I would have been better off learning it from the book. There is only a handful of gym instructors trying to help all of us at once. The training is half fast and sloppy.

When I started to take private self defense lessons, my instructor would ask "Didn't the academy show you this?" I would tell him no and he would shake his head in disbelief.

After the training, one of the instructors would talk to us and briefly go over what we learned. After that we would be dismissed and given time to shower and get ready for our mealtime. The meal was always scheduled after gym. As the gym instructor was finishing his speech, all the guys were inching towards the exits getting ready for the sprint down to the locker room. You had to run

31

as fast as you could down stairs to get to your locker, get naked and grab a spot either in the shower or on line as close to the front of the line as possible. Sure, you could take your time going downstairs, but that would mean waiting on line with nearly two hundred naked men. That's a long, slow line. The only drawback to finishing your shower early was if the naked man line snaked through the locker room through an aisle where your locker was. Now you have to change right next to sweaty, smelly, naked men that you can't help bumping into.

The shower room wasn't any better. Picture a small room with about fifteen showerheads on the walls spread about three feet apart from each other. That's not a pretty picture. In the beginning, most days I just couldn't be bothered with the whole shower experience so I would pour on the deodorant, get dressed and go to meal, but you feel gross the rest of the day. When I finally accepted the whole shower experience, there were two instances that ruined it for me. I'm in the shower for only minutes. In and out. But, one day I see a guy a couple of showerheads away from me urinating. Now there is more water coming out of the showerheads than what the drains can handle, so there is a small puddle constantly covering the shower room floor. This guy is not pissing out oil. If he was, then I wouldn't care because oil and water doesn't mix. But, urine and water is a different story. The idea of standing in urine-water didn't sit too well with me.

I can't really call the second incident an incident but it still had a negative effect on me. What do you think the most uncomfortable, if not the scariest thing that can happen to a man

32

when he's in the shower with other strange men? That's right, I dropped my soap. As soon as the splashing sound came from my soap crashing onto the shower floor, time seemed to move in slow motion. The only thing that I could envision is fourteen other men standing there, watching and waiting for me to bend way over to retrieve my fallen bar.

I calmly put my back against the wall, knelt straight down, kept my eyes forward and felt around for my soap. Now I know I over reacted. I could've just bent down and picked the damn thing up, but hey, why risk it? Better safe than sorry.

That was the final straw. I was through with the shower. I figured that if I could find a way to get out of doing the cals and the run, then I wouldn't need to shower.

One day, before we started the cals, I asked one of the instructors if I could use the bathroom. Upon receiving his permission, I went down to the locker room and sat there until the cals and the run was over. When the class was sent downstairs to get their police equipment, I just walked back upstairs with the rest of the class. Mission accomplished. No cals plus no run equaled no sweating. No sweating meant no shower. Life was good.

CHAPTER 7

With each week that passed, I got more and more accustomed to the whole academy routine even though I would always have trouble staying awake in class during the weeks that we worked the day tour. I never was a morning person and waking up at 6:00 A.M. to catch the train into Manhattan and then catching a cab to the academy would take it's toll on me. But, I wasn't the only one that the instructors would catch sleeping. Several recruits in my company would tend to nod off. After a while, the instructors knew who the sleepers were and it would become sort of a joke among us. We would never get in trouble for sleeping. The instructor would either wake you or have the person next to you give you a nudge and the instructor would let you go wash your face and would ask that you try to stay awake.

I made friends quickly with my fellow classmates and started to get a feel for the ones that I could relate to better. I would sit with the same small group of guys each day. We would have meals together, try to get gym lockers next to each other and study together.

When it came time for the first quarterly exam, we studied every day, either before a class started or during our mealtime. I never established good study habits in school because I always made myself cheat notes, so I figured I would play it safe and make some cheat notes for the academy tests as well. The exam consisted of a hundred multiple-choice questions in Law, a hundred questions in Police Science and a hundred for Social Science.

As it turns out, the questions on the test were so easy that I had to read them several times to make sure that they weren't trick questions. For the remaining quarterly exams, I knew that I would pass them without having to use any help from my little cheat notes.

After the first three exams, I had a ninety-five or higher average in the three classes. Since the average score needed in each class to graduate was a seventy-five, I figured out that if I scored a zero on the Law part, scored a five on the Social Science part and a ten on the Police Science part, I would still have a higher final grade than the mandatory seventy-five. So, I didn't even bother studying for the final exam.

Like I mentioned earlier, old habits are had to break. Here I am doing the minimum necessary just to get by.

The only way to really fail one of these exams is to not show up. My "idiot's test" reference held true throughout the academy. There was one other exam that was given to us. This was the justification exam. It's a test that will determine if we know when, by law, we can fire our service weapons. The test has ten questions in the form of ten situations that requires a cop to either discharge his gun or not. It is mandatory that you score a hundred on this test. We were told that if you don't get a perfect score, then you can go for tutoring and take a make up test. If you fail that then you don't get to graduate. Supposedly. A girl in my company failed the exam THREE times and was then given a private tutoring course and took the test immediately after. Of course she passed the test, graduated, and now has the power to shoot you and she does't even know if she is justified to do so. I learned that the academy talks tough but does not back it up. They can't. The department finds it tough enough to get people to even consider applying for the job that they are not going to fire you that easily.

I realized that I didn't have to give a hundred percent effort and I was still going to graduate. For example, every day during the run, the same girl would drop out after only five or six laps with 'leg cramps'. Her friend would also drop out to help her stretch out those nasty 'leg cramps'. Great scam. But me, like a jerk would do all the laps until I wised up and found my own way to avoid the run.

Before I thought of the bathroom trick, I tried using a medical excuse to get out of the run for one day. One of the weeks that my squad was working the day tour, gym was the first class in the morning. I slowly walked up to the sergeant in charge of the gym class and said "Excuse me sir, but I don't think I can participate in gym today because I woke up with a case of the runs." My thinking was that if someone admits to you that they have the runs, then chances are you will believe that person. "Do you have a note?" he asked. "A note from who?" If I would've known how much of a jackass this guy was before this conversation started, then I wouldn't have been bothered. "The doctor" he replied with a touch of sarcasm. I looked at him with a Perplexed look on my face and said "Sarge, its 7:00 in the morning. I woke up with the runs. When would I have gone to the doctor?" He looked at me like I was a moron and said, "Well, you need a note to be excused." So with that, I ripped out a piece of paper from my notebook and wrote a note excusing myself from gym and handed it to the Sarge. I lost a demerit card for that one. Needless to say, I participated in gym that day and the girl with the leg cramps dropped out again. The funny thing is, she never had to show any type of doctor's note about these chronic leg cramps.

That's because women on this job have it made. Just about every supervisor on the job, in the academy and in the precincts, starting with the sergeants on up, will be extra nice to the female officers and recruits for the chance to get down their pants. A female cop will be given a nice, easy assignment or will be given a choice of assignments before I will. I don't want to sound mean, but even if the girl is ugly it wouldn't matter. Men are dogs. They will take what they can get. I couldn't believe how many married cops have girlfriends on the side, whether it's other female cops or girls that live in the neighborhoods where the cops work. After all, if a guy calls his wife from the precinct and tells her that he made an arrest and will be doing several hours overtime, but is really going out for a good time, how will the wife know? The cop on telephone duty at the precinct will cover for him if the wife calls back looking for him.

In the academy, the male gym instructors score the most. They are usually the good-looking ones with the nice physiques. Also, the workouts are difficult for a lot of the female recruits to do. So here is this good looking, muscular instructor paying special attention to a 'helpless' female recruit and sooner or later there's a little flirting followed by a little touchy feely and before you know it, he's getting what he wants and the girl is 'passing' gym. You know these girls don't need a note for anything. They don't even have to show up.

The day we did boxing was, for lack of a better word, useless. We just put on the gloves, found a partner and boxed. There were no lessons beforehand. Just gear up and go at it. I was lucky enough to find a sparring partner that didn't want to do this as much as me so we faked it. But most guys thought that they were Mike Tyson. Even though we wore mouth pieces, and headgear, noses were bloodied, guys were floored and lips were split.

Watching the girls box against each other was entertaining, if not pathetic. They gave it a good try, but I still couldn't help feeling embarrassed for them. The thing that amused me the most was the fact that the boxing gloves looked extra big when the girls wore them that it reminded me of Charlie Brown and the rest of the Peanuts gang wearing their oversized baseball mitts. I'm not trying to be mean, but let's face it, if you had to rely on most of the women on this job to protect you from physical harm, then you should just put your head between your legs and kiss your ass goodbye! Take myself for example. I'm six feet tall and I weigh 230 lbs. I never met a female cop that would be physically able to stop me in order to protect someone unless she could shoot me. But if the situation doesn't allow for the use of her gun then she's up shit's creek without a paddle.

Now I'm not insinuating that all the men are any more capable of handling themselves in the street. I've worked with a lot of guys that didn't make me feel the least bit secure that they could handle themselves if the shit hit the fan. Let's just say that you know which cops should be on the street on patrol and which cops should be kept in the precinct answering the phones.

CHAPTER 8

The week of training that I was looking forward to finally arrived. My company was off to the firing range in City Island to learn how to use our guns. Weeks before hand, we were shown the two types of guns that the Department issues to cops as their service weapons. One is a Smith and Wesson that is made of metal and has some weight to it. The other is called a Gluck. This gun is made of metal and plastic, so it's a little smaller and lighter than the other one. We were given the chance to hold each one to see which gun felt more comfortable. Remember that the gun you choose is the one you carry for your career. I chose the Smith and Wesson. Most of the girls and some of the smaller guys went with the Glock. It all depends on your personal preference. Both of the guns are equally good. That was the only day we saw our guns until it was the squads turn to go to the firing range for training.

I never fired a gun before so I was excited about this up coming week. Also, just being away from the academy for a week was a welcome relief. I needed such a break from the academy that we could've been sent to a slaughter house for a week and I would've welcomed it with open arms.

On the first day of training, the firearms instructors taught us the ins and outs and the do's and don'ts of gun safety, proper shooting techniques and the maintenance of the guns. We were told true stories of accidental shootings that occur when cops are either careless or just plain stupid when handling their gun. Most accidental shootings occur when a cop is cleaning his or her gun. The instructor also recommended to any of us that have young children or young brothers and sisters at home, to let them see and hold your gun, make sure the gun isn't loaded of course, when you bring it home for the first time and to make sure that they understand how dangerous a gun is. This can help satisfy a child's curiosity about the gun and hopefully the kid won't spend their time trying to find out where you hide your gun. These guns that the Department issues do not have a trigger safety. Pull the trigger and the gunfires. A small child is not strong enough to pull the trigger with one finger. What a child does is they turn the gun around with the barrel facing them and will use both of their thumbs to pull the trigger. This has disaster written all over it. I remember when my sister first came home with her gun, she let me hold it. Even though I was fifteen years old at the time, you are never too old to learn about the destructive power of a gun.

When I woke up on the second morning for gun training, I wasn't feeling too good. I was feeling sluggish and weak. When I arrived to the range, I spent the first fifteen minutes vomiting in the bathroom. I started to get severe dizzy spells and a migraine headache. I informed one of the instructors, and we filled out a sick report and I was sent home. It figures that the one week that I was

41

going to enjoy myself, I would have to get sick. Since I wasn't able to finish my firearms training on time, I would be given a makeup week before the end of the academy training. I wasn't alone. Other recruits that happen to get sick and missed the training or those that failed the firearms training would be joining me during the make up week.

The only drawback to not finishing the gun training on time was that I would end up missing out on a special month of training. Towards the end of the academy training, the recruits are going to be assigned to various precincts throughout the city for one month. This will give us a chance to experience working in a precinct, walking a foot post, issuing summonses, using the police radio, and handling jobs. But those of us that didn't finish any of the required training up to that point or were actually failing academically were not permitted to take part in this month of training. We would continue to report to the academy until the month was over and the rest of the recruits returned to the academy to resume class. The fact that I didn't finish my firearms training and wasn't able to participate in that month's training turned out to be a blessing in disguise for me in a couple of ways. First of all, since there were not that many recruits that stayed behind for the month, we didn't work the normal alternating weeks. We were put into one big squad and worked steady daytime hours for the month. My body will finally get used to working one set of hours without having to change hours the following week. But, the most important benefit to all of this was that the month that was designated to be the training month was December and this included working on New Year's Eve. So, while all of the recruits who were 'lucky' enough to get this training were freezing their asses off, standing on a foot post in the middle of Times Square on New Year's Eve, I spent my night at a KISS concert with my girlfriend at the Meadowlands. I know that when I graduate and show up at my assigned precinct for the first time, I'm going to feel like a fish out of water because I didn't get to experience working in a precinct for that month. But if I was to do it all over again, and had to choose between police training or spending an evening with Gene, Paul, Chris and Ace, and fifty thousand screaming fans, the police training would lose every time.

CHAPTER 9

One of the requirements in the gym class was passing the obstacle course. I can't remember everything that the course consisted of, but I do remember that the first obstacle was scaling a five foot wall. All of the recruits in my company had no problem with this except for one woman who was the oldest person in my company. She was at the age limit acceptable to be starting the academy. She just couldn't get over the wall if her life depended on it. She tried at least six times, but didn't possess the upper body strength to pull herself over. When she finally did get over the wall, so much time had passed that it was impossible for her to finish the course in the required time. Several of us wondered what she was going to do when the day came to pass the course for real. We were warned, just like everything else, that if you don't pass the obstacle course, you don't graduate. By now I knew better. When the day came for us to qualify on the obstacle course, our gym instructor tested her last. But first, after the rest of us ran the course, he had us line up downstairs by the locker room so she could run the course with nobody around except the instructor. Miraculously, she passed. Maybe it was an act of God that enabled her to muster up enough strength to get over that wall and pass the course when it really counted. What made it worse was that the instructor yelled "Come on, you can do it! Don't stop!" loud enough for all of us to hear it. I guess this was supposed to make us believe that she was actually doing this legitimately. If things like this were going to happen every time someone was at a risk of failing something, then why bother testing any of us? Just pass us all and save us the hard work.

I pray that the time never comes that a cop is in serious trouble and has to depend on this woman to scale a fence or a wall to rescue them. It could be a matter of life or death and it's not fair to put anyone at this risk.

It just doesn't seem fair that those of us that are physically and academically capable to pass the required training have to watch those that can't do it get special 'attention' in order to reach graduation. My belief is that you can either do what is required or you can't. Plain and simple. But, it will continue to be like this until the Department can find a way to attract enough people on a daily basis to apply for the job that they can afford to weed out the weak. This would require a nice pay increase and that will never happen.

CHAPTER 10

One person in my company quit before the eight months was complete. I don't know the exact number of people that quit during the training, but it was rumored to be about two hundred.

Sixteen people quit in one day alone. That was the day the academy was giving the surprise urine drug test. My squad was working the day tour and when we showed up in the morning, we were corralled like cattle outside the academy. We were told that there were not going to any classes today because we were going to be drug tested.

The name of the test is the Dole test. The drugs that the department tests for are cocaine, marijuana and other opiates. If you test positive, then you are fired. The expression used is that you 'doled out'. When the announcement about the Dole test was made, ten people from squad A quit on the spot. They didn't even bother taking it. When the B squad started showing up for the afternoon shift, then people from that squad quit.

The department was smart in choosing the day for the test. They tested us on the first day after the Yankees won their first World Series of the nineties. The department probably figured that some of the recruits went out and celebrated the Yankees victory.

Well, they were right. Not only did those recruits quit, but a number of others doled out. I can't understand how you can throw away months of training like that.

The Police Department stands by a strict 'no tolerance' policy when it comes to drug use. You could have one day left to retire, but if you get dole tested and fail, then you are terminated and lose everything. Your pension, benefits, everything. It's a very strict policy, but it's necessary because the last thing the public needs is a cop on a patrol high on drugs.

Cops are chosen at random for the Dole test throughout their careers. When you are notified, you have to go take the test right away. No questions asked. My partner and I were on patrol during a midnight tour when we were called into our precinct at six in the morning because the notification came in for my partner to take the Dole test. My partner had to change out of his uniform and drive into Queens where the test is given. If he had plans in the morning after work, then those plans had to wait.

Since you are chosen at random, you have no idea when your name will pop up. My sister worked her first ten years without getting called, and then she got notified twice in one week.

The one thing that is legal and that cops do a lot of is drink. No matter what shift you work, there will always be a few cops who stay after work and hang out in the precinct parking lot with a couple of six packs. I don't know how the cops that I work with on the midnight shift can hang out at 8:00 A.M. in the lot and drink. The cops that work the 4 P.M. to 12 A. M. tour will be off to the bar after work. That's called working a 4 to 4 shift. You end up hanging out until 4:00 in the morning, go home and sleep into the afternoon, wake up and go right back to work. Sounds like a lot of fun. I'll pass.

A lot of cops drink due to the high stress level of the job. The daily pressure of risking your life combined with the constant pressure from the supervisors to maintain a high level of summonses takes its toll on you. It's tough to try to talk to friends or loved ones about the job because they don't know what it's like. Also, it's tough to raise a family on a cops salary so a lot of cops have money problems. A lot of cops try to drink their problems away. Next thing you know the cop is an alcoholic. There are support groups set up within the department that offers counseling, but it's up to the cop to take the first step.

If the pressure of the job combined with financial troubles get to be too much for a cop to handle, then the next step is suicide. More cops are killed each year with their own gun then are killed in the line of duty.

There are other solutions available besides blowing your brains out. A cop with a drinking problem can come forward and tell a supervisor and arrangements will be made to get that cop help. Either you will be taken off the street while you receive help or you will be sent to the "farm" to sober up.

That's great, but if your drinking leads to a drug problem or have been addicted to drugs for a while and have been lucky enough not to be dole tested, you can't come forward to get help. You will be fired immediately. That's because drugs are illegal. But we are human and make mistakes. If you have a drug problem and want help so you can keep your job to support your family, I feel that you should be able to tell the department and receive the same help as an alcoholic. But, the only options available to a cop addicted to drugs are to either quit, work until you get dole tested, which can take years, or end up killing someone.

Why is it that you read about pro athletes and movie stars getting busted time after time, but are given countless chances to get help so they can resume their careers, but the average "jerk" with arguable one of the most dangerous and stressful jobs in the world can't get a second chance? I love the excuse that is used when a young pro athlete gets caught with drugs. "He didn't know how to handle the sudden fame and all the money he was exposed to." I'm sure you've heard that one. They have got to be kidding me. I would love to see how hard it is to handle fame and fortune. I've handled wrestling and fighting for my life with criminals that are high on drugs and out of their minds and all they want to do is kill me, so I think fame and fortune would be a breeze. The next celebrity that gets caught with drugs and blames their rich and famous lifestyle should be dressed up in a cops uniform and dropped off in the middle of the South Bronx at 1:00 in the morning. That cop uniform is like a big blue target to some of the maniacs out there. I guarantee that the celebrity will run back to their fame and fortune lifestyle with a new found respect of just how lucky they are and will think twice about risking it all for drugs.

If the mayor and other high ranking city officials knew how much drinking cops do while on patrol during the holidays, they would be shocked. Maybe they do know and choose to look the other way at it.

Being on patrol during New Years Eve was all about drinking. As long as you were lucky enough not to be sent down to Times Square, you would go on patrol with your partner and get "happy." My partner and I would keep a bottle of vodka and a container of o.j. in our personal cars and would make routine visits to grab a refill. When you work the midnight shift, it's just the two of you celebrating the coming of the New Year, so you have to make it count. My partner and I celebrated every New Year's Eve that we worked together. Not only was it fun, but I found it much easier dealing with the public when I'm a little tipsy. The only worry is the risk of getting caught by a supervisor even though some of the bosses were in on the drinking too.

CHAPTER 11

I never thought that the big day would come. Eight months have come and gone, all the training was completed and all the tests were passed. It is now graduation day at Madison Square Garden. The Mayor, the Police Commissioner and a number of city officials were going to be on hand for this joyous occasion.

Tickets were available for us to buy in the academy so we could invite our families and friends.

A couple of days before the big day, a PBA delegate came to the academy to talk to us about the graduation ceremony. He asked us to tell the people that we are inviting, not to boo or cheer for the mayor when he is introduced. Since the PBA is not happy with the contract negotiations and the fact that the N.Y.C. P.D. is the largest in the country and yet among the lowest paid, they figure if the mayor receives a no response from the audience when he is introduced, it will have a bigger impact on him instead of booing him. I never understood that one, but when he was introduced, most of the crowd gave him a mixed reception. So much for the strategy.

51

We are all decked out in our nice dress uniforms that we wear for special department occasions like funerals for slain officers or promotional ceremonies. We marched into the garden to the tune of New York, New York as all of our friends and family members looked on and applauded. Eventually, the graduating class of 1996 were all standing at attention in front of our seats waiting for old blue eyes to finish singing the song that only he can sing.

Overall, it really was a nice ceremony that was highlighted by the mayor giving us the policeman' oath. It was a happy and exciting day for all of us, but also a sad one. Most of the people that I befriended in my eight months in the academy, I was never going to see again. We were going to report to our assigned precincts and get on with our lives as police officers. Sometimes at parades or other details in the city, I would bump into some of the cops that I graduated with, but it was rare.

After we recited the oath, we threw our caps in the air and hugged and congratulated each other. When the ceremony was over. I met up with my family and my girlfriend and received hugs and kisses for my accomplishment. My dad treated us all to a nice dinner on my behalf and my sister and her husband gave me as much advice as they could to help prepare me for my first day at my new precinct.

"Don't worry if the other cops don't talk to you right away. You're the new guy, and the veteran cops are going to feel you out, to try to see what kind of person you are," she said. "What do you mean?" I asked. "They want to see if you are the type of guy that will run to the supervisor for every little thing, or to see if you are a team player and can be trusted" her husband added. "Don't worry, you'll be fine my sister said." Just don't do too much and make yourself stand out. Just do enough to be somewhere in the middle of the pack." I really didn't understand what they were saying, but I would find out in time.

About a week before graduation, we were given a sheet of paper to write down the top three precincts that we would like to work in and the department would try to accommodate us. That sheet of paper was called the "dream sheet", and for good reason. You had to be dreaming to think you would get the precinct you asked for. My three picks were all in Queens. I wanted to work close to home, and I wanted to work in a nice, quiet area. I though of Staten Island, but it's too far to commute.

Only the recruits that either had a relative on the job in a high ranking position or new someone in that capacity could have some strings pulled for them so they could get their pick on the dream sheet.

A lot of my classmates couldn't understand why I wanted to work in quiet areas and not where there is a lot of action. "You'll never learn the job in a slow command," they would say to me with a snotty tone in their voice. Instead of arguing, I would just nod my head in agreement. What a bunch of jackasses, I would say to myself. What do they think this is? Rocket science? I have twenty years to learn this job and I'll get paid the same no matter what area I work in.

The one thing that the academy did teach me is that I don't like working the day tour or the 4 x 12 tour. I wanted to work the midnight shift. I wanted to be on patrol at three in the morning with not a whole hell of a lot going on. So where do I get assigned? The South Bronx. The armpit of the city.

I didn't even know how to get to the South Bronx. I was there once when I was seven years old and my old man took me to a Yankee game. That's about it.

When I told my family where my precinct was, my mom cried and my brother in-law laughed. "Good luck" he said as he patted me on the back.

My brother in-law did me the favor of driving me to the precinct so I can get an idea of what the precinct is like and to see the surrounding neighborhood.

What a shit hole! I never saw so much garbage on the streets and on the sidewalks in my life. There were rats the size of cats running in and out of abandoned buildings, and if I saw one pile of dog shit on the sidewalk. I saw a thousand. Trying to walk down the block avoiding all the shit was like walking through a mine field. This area really was the armpit of the city. The city would be better off dropping a bomb on it and starting over. When I started to work the midnight shift, the only time I saw a car with white people in it, they were either lost or buying drugs.

One other recruit from my company was assigned to the same precinct with me. Bruce was a down to earth guy who grew up in Manhattan and is a few years older than me and we got along great. We still get together for a few beers to this day. The fact that we had each other to talk to and help each other out made the whole experience a little easier. All together, fifteen recruits were assigned to this command.

CHAPTER 12

All the recruits assigned to the Bronx had to report to Fordham University for an orientation and an introduction to the Bronx. We were seated in groups according to the precinct that we were in and listened to different police personnel take their turns telling us how great the Bronx is and how fortunate we all are to be assigned to this borough.

I'm sure that there are some very nice areas of the Bronx, but I have already seen where I'm working and the last thing I needed to hear was their bullshit, so I didn't pay much attention.

When I walked into the precinct for my first day of work, I had the same feeling of nervousness and uncertainty that I had every time I started a new school year. As I entered through the front doors and walked towards the staircase that led to the locker room, I could feel the stare of every cop that I passed along the way. I met up with Bruce and together we searched for empty lockers. We checked all three locker rooms but we would have had a better chance searching for Big Foot. You would think that a precinct would prepare itself for the additional number of rookies it receives from every graduating class. But I guess that is too much to ask for.

When Bruce and I finally found an empty locker, we still had one problem. Bruce, myself, and one of the other rookies all needed lockers. For the first three months the three of us shared one locker. It was definitely an uncomfortable situation that we had to tolerate until new lockers were brought in or some of the present ones were vacated.

On a day that I arrived to work a little earlier than usual, I decided to look around the precinct to see if I could find a locker. I wound up in the basement boiler room where I found a locker full of old pots and pans. I dumped the stuff out, strapped the locker to a hand truck and proceeded to carry it up three flights of stairs to the locker room where I had a nice spot waiting for it. I nestled it into place, cleaned it up and had myself my very own locker. I offered Bruce the opportunity to be my locker mate, and he gladly accepted. A week later, Bruce got a locker of his own.

Our first six months in the precinct were considered our training months. We were assigned a sergeant and two veteran officers that would "baby-sit" us in that time. They would teach us all the aspects of the job, such as making and processing arrests, filling out department paper work and handling jobs in general.

Since most of the veterans wouldn't really talk to rookies, we had to stick together until we found our nitch and were accepted by the others. For the training months, we were scheduled to work from 6:00 P.M. to 2:00 in the morning. We were give these hours so the 4 x 12 squad and the midnight squad would both benefit from the extra manpower.

Our daily assignment was walking a footpost. We were told to issue summonses and listen to the police radios for jobs that were close enough for us to respond to. We would walk the designated posts in teams of two, so Bruce and I asked our training sergeant if we could be sent out on patrol together all the time.

Let me tell you that the experiences we had in our first weeks on a footpost were things that the academy never prepared us for or even mentioned to us. Most people don't realize the daily crap that cops have to put up with everyday because it doesn't make the newspapers.

How many people would know that every time a cop enters an apartment building in the projects, he is at risk of being hit by an object thrown off the roof or thrown out of an apartment window? I've had chunks of cement, six inch nails, and used diapers thrown at me, just to name a few. Our training officers warned us about this. The expression cops use is "air mail." Bruce was hit in the arm with a brick that was tossed off the roof of a seventeen-story window. He's lucky that his arm wasn't broken, only badly bruised.

But I hate to think what the outcome would have been if the brick had hit him in the head.

The one thing that the training officers warned us of is falling dogs. Myself and the other rookies laughed at what we thought was a joke. But, the training officers went on to explain that during the summer months, there are people that bet on dog fights that they organize in the projects. The fights are held on the rooftops and the losing dog is thrown off the roof. I was still a skeptic after I heard this. Until one day, while walking a footpost, a call came over the radio for a dog stuck on a fence. It was right around the corner from Bruce and I so we ran to the scene and saw a Pitbull impaled on a wrought iron fence. The impact nearly tore the poor animal completely in half. I ran to the corner store and bought a disposable camera and took several photos. "My friends will never believe this one," I said to Bruce. I asked the central dispatcher to have sanitation respond and about a half hour later, a garbage truck pulled up and proceeded to take the dog away. Now I know why the majority of the dogs I see people walking in this neighborhood are Pitbulls and Rottweilers. All these dogs are to most of these bastards are future contenders. The stray dogs that I see roaming the streets are better off than these poor animals. Some dog owners actually mix gunpowder in the dog food to make the dogs more nasty and irritable. I can't imagine what these dogs went through every time they went to the bathroom. I would be one nasty S.O.B. too.

CHAPTER 13

My first six months were exciting, eye opening, embarrassing, and just plain fun all rolled up together. I was anxious to get to work and see what the day would bring. When it came to issuing summonses though, I heeded my sisters advice and gave an average of fifteen to twenty summonses a month. Even though the training sergeant told us that he expected at least thirty a month from each of us, I felt it was more important that I looked like a team player to the veteran cops instead of making this sergeant happy. Cops notice who the kiss asses are and which rookies are more level headed. Besides, when you give the number of summonses that is asked of you, they end up wanting more. If our supervisor asks for thirty summonses and you consistently give thirty, the next thing you know, they want forty. Some of the rookies were giving between fifty and sixty summonses a month. Not only are they not using any discretion, but they are making enemies among the veterans even if the other cops don't say anything to them. But eventually, one veteran will have a talk with the ticket loving rookie and set him or her straight on the way things are done. If that rookie doesn't change their ways, the next step will be either turning their locker over or completely alienating that rookie among all the cops in the command.

Needless to say, I continued giving my fifteen summonses a month. Most of the summonses I gave were parking summonses. But I used a ton of discretion. If a car had handicapped plates, and was parked illegally, I wouldn't issue it a summons. I figured the owner has enough problems to deal with without getting a lousy summons from me. An easy summons to give in the South Bronx is one for drinking beer in public. I couldn't bring myself to write a summons for some thing that I did and still do to this day. Also, most of these people are going to live and die without ever leaving the South Bronx. All they have to do with their time is drink their beer, so I let them do it in peace.

Some of the rookies were heartless. In the course of conversation, I told one of the other rookies my policy on not issuing parking summonses to cars that have handicapped plates and his response was "It doesn't matter to me. The fact that someone is handicapped affects me how?" I knew right then and there that I was dealing with an asshole.

There are good reasons to issue drinking summonses. First, you are allowed to do a search of the person. This can lead to finding drugs or weapons. Also, when you do a name check in the computer, an active warrant could be out on that person.

I would say that the odds were one in twenty that you would end up with something more than just a beer summons but there were some rookies who were looking for the action and the pat on the back for making a good arrest, so they issued summonses to anyone they came across that was drinking a beer. I remember one of the rookies gave a beer summons to an eighty-year-old man. This poor guy has lived his entire life in the same neighborhood and isn't bothering anyone and this hot shot feels the unrelenting urge to write him a summons. Maybe I'm wrong, but I just don't see the point.

To me, letting someone off with a warning is more satisfying than issuing that person a summons. Of course, if the person acts up and disrespects me, well then, they asked for it. In my career, I issued a total of three beer drinking summonses and all three were under the direct order from a supervisor.

The problem is, that the only thing the department cares about is summonses. All the crime reduction that you read about is nice, but the fact is, that making arrest doesn't make the city any money. In fact, it costs the city money with all the overtime cops make when they process an arrest. Summonses, on the other hand, make the city money. The more the better. I could make fifty arrests a month, but if my summons count is low, I'll hear about if from a supervisor. Each cop in my precinct was only required to make four arrests all year. That alone should tell you what the city thinks about arrests.

We were told that there is no such thing as a quota when it came to how many summonses you give. What a bunch of bullshit that is. I've known a lot of cops that were either transferred from one squad to another or transferred to another command as punishment because their summons count was consistently low.

Whenever you are driving somewhere and you come across cops doing a checkpoint, it's because the summons count for the neighborhood precinct is down for the month and the commanding officer wants to give an instant boost to the numbers. So when you find yourself stuck in traffic due to one of these checkpoints and you ask yourself, "Don't these cops have anything better to do?" the answer is "yes, we do but we have no choice." I never met a cop that enjoyed doing a checkpoint.

I was doing a checkpoint that led to my first arrest. The driver that I stopped didn't have his license on him. When I entered his name in the computer, it showed that his license was suspended. My training sergeant instructed me to put the handcuffs on him and take him back to the command. When I saw how much paperwork was necessary to fill out for an arrest, I vowed to never make another arrest again. But since I knew that wasn't possible, I decided t learn the arrest process from start to finish as fast as I could.

I didn't want to have to be dependant on anyone for help. Even though cops in the precinct were nice enough to guide me until my training officers arrived. After about eight months, I was able to process and arrest in under an hour. I had veterans coming to me, asking to help them with their arrests. Even though processing an arrest became a piece of cake for me, I never liked making arrests. The thing about it that I didn't like was that eventually you would have to go to court to speak to the assistant district attorney about it. You had no idea when that day was. So, at any time, you can receive the court date. If you had plans for that day, they had to be cancelled. The one thing that I didn't want was for this job to interfere with my personal life.

When I learned that after the training months are over and we are put into squads, that the required number of arrests is four a year, I was delighted. I knew after my first arrest that I didn't like making arrests and would try to avoid making them unless it was absolutely necessary.

The jails are so overcrowded, that the person I arrest is usually back on the streets in a couple of days anyway. There are some Perps that are arrested so many times that we let them fingerprint themselves. Some of them do it better than some of the cops! Then there are those cops that will arrest anybody. An easy way for these cops to make an arrest is to enter the lobby of an apartment building and question anyone that happens to be hanging out in the lobby. If that person doesn't live there or doesn't know anyone that lives in the building, then they are arrested for criminal trespassing. IF the person claims that he knows someone in the building, then the cops are supposed to go to the apartment to see if that person is telling the truth. Most cops won't do this. They just make the arrest and that person is shit out of luck.

I asked one of the cops that likes to make his arrest this way." What if someone went to call for their friend, and their friend isn't home, and as they were leaving, you guys stop him?" The cop said to me "Hey, in the wrong place at the wrong time":. That's fucked up.

A lot of the people that are arrested for criminal trespassing are homeless people looking for a place to sleep. Some of the homeless that are brought into the precinct stink so bad it makes me gag.

Some of the homeless that these cops arrest have had body lice, hepatitis and AIDS. Not only are they arrested for criminal trespassing, but you are bound to find some crack or marijuana on them. Even if someone has a crack pipe with nothing else but some residue on it, they will be arrested. As far as I'm concerned, it's just not worth the risk. I know that cops have families, and bills need to be paid, so they need the overtime, but I would rather work a second job instead of dealing with disease infested crack heads.

The only thing that bothers me about this and it shouldn't, is that these cops will then brag about how many arrests they make. They assume that the more arrest you make, no matter how petty, the better cop you are. It's a shame how hungry an ego can be.

65

CHAPTER 14

The only way to get away with doing the minimum is if you're a woman. I've said it before and I'll say it again, woman have it made on this job.

I'll never forget the day that I walked into the precinct with two other rookies, Pete and Denise before our tour started. Pete was a real nice guy, who was married with a newborn baby. He escaped the N.Y.P.D. to become a fireman after only two years on the job. Denise was an attractive young woman who knew how to use her looks to her advantage. I would always see Denise flirting with most of the supervisors in the command. As we walked past the desk sergeant, he yells out "Mike, Pete! You two guys are going to be on a footpost where we have been getting a lot of complaints about drug dealing." We just shrugged our shoulders and nodded. I really didn't care until the Sarge said "Denise, dear. What would you like to do?" The wimpy, feminine tone he used made me feel embarrassed to have him as part of the male gender. "I don't know" Denise said. "I'll get back to you after I change" and she walked away with a little extra shake to her ass. As we walked upstairs, Pete asked me, "How come the Sarge didn't ask us what we wanted to do?" "Because we don't have tits and a vagina" was my answer.

Another incident that burns me up is about a month into training, another rookie and I get called into the command along with one of our training officers. As we walk in we are met by our Captain who is standing there with a female rookie cop and a female complainant who was assaulted by her boyfriend and wanted him arrested "Go to this address and ask for Juan" the captain said. "If he's home, arrest him." He added. "No problem" our training officer replied. But, the captain then added, "When you bring him in, Michelle is going to take the arrest." The other rookie and I looked at each other dumbfounded. Apparently, Michelle hasn't made her first arrest yet. Wouldn't she want to be the one to make her first arrest? It would end up taking me over two months to make my first arrest and nobody offered me any handouts.

Anyway, the three of us head over to Juan's' apartment and me and the other rookie just don't have our hearts in it. How could we when we already knew that we were doing the work for someone else? When we rang the bell, a six and a half foot, two hundred and fifty pound monster opens the door. This guy was built like a brick shit house. "Uh, is Juan home?" the training officer asked with a hope in his voice that the answer would be no. The good thing was that we didn't have a search warrant. Even if Juan is home and hercules here says that he's not, we are not allowed to enter the apartment to

67

look around. All three of us are hoping that this guys skull isn't full of muscle and he doesn't say yes.

"Na, he ain't here." That was music to our ears. We let out a collective sigh, apologized for bothering him and left. As we headed back to the station house, I said "Do you guys realize that if this guy would've been dumb enough to say that Juan was home, that there was no way that he would've let us arrest Juan peacefully. And on top of that, Michelle would get credit for the arrest without lifting a finger!"

CHAPTER 15

Our training sergeant asked for two volunteers to work at the church in the neighborhood that held parties every Saturday night for the rest of the summer months. In the churches' recreation room, events like wedding receptions, sweet sixteen parties and birthday parties were booked during the summer. Our commanding officer wanted to have two cops there just to show a police presence to make sure things didn't get out of hand.

As an incentive to get two volunteers, out training Sgt. Said that whoever volunteers will be given Thursday and Friday nights off. That's a lot better than the Wednesday and Thursday nights we had off during our training months, so I jumped at the chance to have Friday nights off.

The first party that I worked at was a Mexican wedding. There were two security guards hired by the church to work the door. They weren't really security guards, just two decent guys from the neighborhood that offered to help out.

One thing that we had to watch out for was people from the street trying to sneak their way into the party trying to grab a free meal. But, the other thing was that we had to search the party guests as they entered the party. I never attended a wedding where I was searched, so I felt a little uncomfortable doing this.

The first person I searched was a young guy that had a napsack with him. I opened his napsack and pulled out a switchblade knife. That uncomfortable feeling I had left me in a hurry. We weren't going to arrest anyone or issue summonses for the weapons, but we confiscated them. I have no idea what possesses a person to feel the need to arm themselves at a wedding reception but I have a pretty impressive knife collection thanks to these parties.

Some of the guys thought they were slick and would try to hide there weapons in the surrounding bushes before we searched them, but I would find there weapons and then watch them try to find them after the party was over. I would calmly walk up to them and show them their weapon and say "Looking for this?" They would just shake their heads no and scurry off.

Some of the weapons that I confiscated were razors, ice picks, screwdrivers that were filed down to a point and brass knuckles. Throughout the course of the night, me, the other rookie, and the two security guards would pick the weapons that we wanted and the rest of them we threw down the sewer.

The biggest advantage that volunteering for this gig was the fact that there was a firehouse right across the street from the church. My old man always told me to stop into a firehouse when I'm on patrol and I could have dinner with the guys. When I mentioned this to the other rookie that I was with, he was too scared of getting into trouble so he didn't want to do it. Besides, we were offered food from the parties in the church, but I can only eat so much rice and beans before I get sick of it.

When I knocked on the door to the firehouse, I asked the fireman that answered if they had room for one more at dinner. "Sure we do," he said with a big grin on his face. "Come back around 8:00. We're having pasta." I ran over to the store and bought a pound of butter cookies to bring the firemen as a token of my appreciation. I just felt like it was the right thing to do. Also, I planned on asking them for dinner next Saturday, and I don't want them to think that I'm an ungrateful grub.

I showed up at 8:00 with my cookies and the firemen invited me in and added the cookies to their deserts. They gave me a tour of the firehouse and I couldn't believe the accommodations the firehouse had. They had cable t.v. with H.B.O., a game room that included a pool table, a ping pong table and video games. The firemen built a deck in the yard that was equipped with a huge bar-b-que and a dartboard. It was their home away from home.

The pasta dinner was fabulous. These guys really know how to cook. The dinner included meatballs, sausage, and garlic bread. For dessert, there was homemade apple pie and the box of cookies that I brought.

After dinner, I talked to the firemen about trivial things like the difference between the two jobs. I was amazed at how many firemen started out as cops. I told them that my father was a cop and that he rolled over to the F.D. They advised me to follow in his footsteps. But, the concept of running into a burning building doesn't sit well with me, so I'll stay where I am.

After enjoying a few after dinner beers with the guys, I walked back to the church already looking forward to next weeks meal. And from this day on, I will always be envious of a fireman's job. Except for the fire fighting part, of course.

CHAPTER 16

I was notified to work the rally that was organized for Mr. Abner Luima. He was the unfortunate victim of police brutality that took place in the bathroom of a police station when a cop sodomized him with the handle of a plunger.

I remember when the story first made the news. I was sure that there was no way that a cop could do such a disgusting and brutal act. Myself, along with many other cops, were confident that the real truth would be revealed during the course of the trial. But, then came the shocking confession by the accused officer and a dark cloud was cast over the entire police department that could take the department years to recover from.

The rally was to be held on the Manhattan side of the Brooklyn Bridge. The protesters were going to march from Brooklyn across the bridge into Manhattan where a podium was set up with a microphone so the civil leaders and other politicians could address the crowd about police brutality and improve the relations between the police and the minority communities.

The only solution that I could come up with is to have minority cops working in minority neighborhoods, and have the white cops work in the white neighborhoods. This way, when the police need to arrest someone, the community leaders can't cry racism. But that will never happen and people would still try to play the race card anyway.

As all the cops arrived in the morning, we were lined up and waited for instructions from the inspector in charge of the day. Inspector is the rank after captain, so it's a pretty powerful rank within the department. The inspector we had on this day was a real prick that treated cops like shit. He had about thirty-five years on the job and looked as though he should've retired al long time

75

ago. Like I said earlier, the problem with a lot of bosses is that they forget that at one time they too started out as simple cops, but once they get promoted, the new found power goes right to their head and they think they are better than you. In my time on the job, I lived by the rule that you respect the rank, but not the man. I'll salute him and show him the respect that his rank deserves but I will not let anyone, not even the chief of police, talk to me in a way that I felt was demeaning or belittling to me. If any supervisor wanted to reprimand me, then it should be kept on a professional level.

The one time that I was being yelled at by a captain for something that I did that he didn't like, he started to get nasty and call me names like dummy and useless. I calmly said to him "Sir, with all due respect, I have a father to talk to me like that. I don't need you to do it," and I walked away. For me, no job is worth sacrificing my pride and dignity.

Anyway, we were all lined up as the inspector paced back and forth in front of us sizing us up. The first thing that the inspector warned us about is that these people are very frustrated and angry with the police and will yell at you, curse at you, and will try to instigate you. "I don't want anyone of you to take police action unless that person is becoming violent," he said. The inspector carried on about showing a good image today and informed us on the time frame of the rally. Before he dismissed us to our posts, he warned us that he didn't want to catch any of us removing our hats in public. "If I catch any officer removing his or her hat, I will call your command and you will have a C.D. waiting for you!" Those were pretty much his exact words.

After a minute or so, I thought about what he just said and came to the conclusion that we are at a rally for a human being that had a wooden stick rammed into his rectum by a cop, and this moron is worried that I might be seen in public without my hat on and that it will send out a bad image to the public? I don't get it.

The cops were stationed about twenty feet apart from each other along the police barriers that outlined the marching route. As far as I could tell, we all had our hats on.

I was about fifty feet from the podium and couldn't believe how many people were marching past me and gathering in front of the stage. I stood my ground as the protesters yelled and cursed at me. Some of them even waved a plunger saying to me "Stick it right here, officer. You would love to stick this in my ass wouldn't you, you pig!" as he stuck his ass out and pointed to it. Since the parade was on my day off, I was working the entire day on overtime so I couldn't care less what these fools said to me. I just smiled, waved at him, and said ""Have a nice day Mr. Overtime."" Because if it wasn't for these people wanting a rally, I wouldn't be here getting paid for this.

I stood there all day, kept my hat on, and earned time and a half to listen to a bunch of drunks accuse me of being a racist. That was the easiest money I ever made. The whole situation was more amusing to me that it was insulting.

Now I can understand and even accept the fact that a lot of people are fed up with police brutality and are taking this opportunity to vent their frustrations. But why do they have to involve their young children? I had several small children, some barely old enough to walk, come over to me throughout the course of the day holding plungers. I'm sure that these kids didn't go into their bathrooms and grab the plunger to prepare themselves for the rally. The sad part is that these kids have no idea why they are here or what they are doing, but I guess their parents are trying to send some kind of message. The only message that I get from this is that the parents want their kids to grow up with the same feeling of distrust and a lack of respect for the police. With ongoing ignorance like this, how can there be any hope of achieving the type of relationship that is wanted between the police and the community?

I smiled at the children that approached me with their plungers because all they wanted to do was to show off the "toy" that was given to them to play with. When I looked into their innocent faces, it made me feel sad to think that these kids are going to grow up being taught to be just as ignorant and angry as their parents. It's a vicious cycle with no end in sight.

As the speakers took their turns saying their speeches, the crowd grew bigger and louder. "No justice, no peace!" That expression was the common battle cry used during any injustices committed against minorities by the police. Every speaker started their speech by screaming this expression out several times. After a while, I found that I was saying it to myself in my head. It was like having a bad song stuck in your head that you can't get rid of but at the same time you can't stop singing.

There were dozens of speakers but they all pretty much said the same thing. "Police brutality must stop!" "We don't want to be treated like animals!" "We demand respect!" Hey, that's all fine and dandy, but when the rally was over and the people cleared out, the amount of garbage left behind was ridiculous. There was even garbage in the treetops. I find it ironic that these people are demanding respect yet they have no respect for themselves or the communities in which they live.

No matter how many protests and marches against police brutality are organized, the people involved never fail to make themselves look like uneducated, and unsophisticated loud mouths. There is the expression "practice what you preach." If someone wants to be respected then they should know how to give respect in return.

Overall, the day went without any major incident. The people vented their anger and I guess they felt that they got their point across on the issue. I even learned some new expletives that were thrown my way.

But the most satisfying part of the whole day for me was that I took my hat off several times throughout the afternoon to air out my head and I never got caught.

CHAPTER 17

Toward the end of the training months, I had made a lot of friends among the other cops. The cops on the day tour asked me to work days, and the 4 x 12 cops suggested that I work with them on the afternoon shift. But I had my heart set on the midnight tour.

During our last week of training, our sergeant told us that there were a couple of openings available on the midnights. I volunteered and was put into a midnight squad effective immediately. Hardly anybody will volunteer for the late shift because not too many people can sleep during the day. Also, if you have small children at home, sleeping during the day would almost be impossible. I didn't have their problem.

All the shifts were made up of three squads. The morning shift was squads B1, B2, and B3. The afternoon squad was C1, 2 and 3, and the midnights started with an A. I was assigned to squad A2.

The cops in my squad were a laid back bunch of guys that didn't get too carried away with police work. They knew how to pace themselves and do just enough to keep the bosses happy without killing themselves. That's my kind of squad. There were two cops in particular that I became very close to. Officer's Joe and Frank are two veterans that have been partners for about five years. Joe had about seventeen years on the job and Frank had about thirteen. Once they realized that I wasn't your typical rookie that loved to be in the middle of the action, they took me under their wing and showed me the ropes.

Who would've thought that one day I would take part in saving Franky's life? I sometimes ask myself that if I had never volunteered for the midnights, would Franky still have survived that heart attack on that horrible night?

My first several months on the midnights, I was given all the shitty assignments to do. I expected that because I was the new guy and I wasn't a female. IF there was a crime scene that needed to be guarded, I got it. If there was a dead body to be guarded until the ambulance came, I got it. I didn't mind because I was working the hours that I wanted and knew that eventually another academy class would graduated we would get brand new rookies on the midnights. That would give me some seniority. I know I just told you that I didn't mind the shitty assignments, but that's not entirely true. Certain jobs like guarding a dead body or sitting in the hospital guarding a sick or injured prisoner can have its downfalls. You might be asking yourself what could possibly go wrong doing either one of these tasks. Well, I'll start with guarding the dead body or D.O.A. as it's referred to. Basically, you're sitting with the dead body waiting for the medical examiner to show up to see if there are any signs of foul play. But, it's not always peaches and cream. First, there is the smell to contend with. Sometimes a D.O.A. is an elderly person that lived alone and isn't discovered until a few weeks go by and the neighbors start complaining about a strange odor in the hallways. As soon as you enter the lobby you can smell it.

Then there is the type of D.O.A. either by natural causes, murder, suicide, accident or drug overdose. Some D.O.A.'s can be very messy. The worst D.O.A. I had wasn't messy or smelly. It was a two month old baby. To me that just doesn't seem right. I'm not going to go into details about it. It's just my way of letting the little guy rest in peace.

But, what I will gladly talk about is the D.O.A. that my good friend Bruce got stuck with. We were still in training when I heard a call come over that a dead body was washed up on the shore by the Triborough Bridge. A few hours later I hear Bruce's voice come over the radio and say "Central, do you have an e.t.a. on the ambulance because high tide is coming in awfully quick."

I laughed when I heard this and didn't really give it much thought for the rest of the night until I spoke to Bruce. I spoke to him the next day about it and Bruce told me that as he was standing on the shore watching the tide come in, he realized that the body could float away. So, he attempted to move the body further up the beach, but when he grabbed it, he said the smell that came out of it almost made him puke. So, with some quick thinking and a little ingenuity, he untied the corpses shoelaces and tied them to a branch that was half buried in the sand. Now that the body was "anchored" he could relax a little bit until the examiner arrived. But, this is nothing compared to what could have happened a little earlier on. Bruce told me that when he was assigned the D.O.A., the desk sergeant gave him a patrol car so he could drive himself to the scene. Since Bruce couldn't see the body from the street, he parked the car and walked down to the shore. A few minutes later the patrol sergeant shows up to see if Bruce is okay. The Sarge tells Bruce that he doesn't have to stay on the shore, he can sit and wait in the car. Bruce decides to stay on the beach. At that time Bruce didn't know that he made a career saving decision. If Bruce had elected to sit in the car, he would have sat there while the tide came in and carried the body away along with Bruce's career. You see, when cops graduate the academy, they are on probation for two years. That means the department can fire you for messing up and the P.B.A. can't help you.

If the tide carries that body away, it's on Bruce's head. The harbor patrol would have to be called, along with aviation to send its helicopters. It would have been a major cluster fuck. Once the higher ups find out that it's because of a rookie, they would have crucified Bruce. Sometimes the smallest decisions in life turn out to the biggest.

***

Guarding hospitalized prisoners is not hard at all. All you do is find yourself a nice comfortable chair, get a sandwich and some reading material, and sit your ass outside the Perps room. Sounds simple, right? It is. But what do you think the main problem is for a cop that works the midnight shift and has to sit in one spot for eight hours is? If you said staying awake, you would be right. Don't get me wrong, there were times that I would request to be sent to the hospital. If I knew that my partner wasn't coming in that night or was assigned to a detail, rather than work with someone else I would ask if there are any hospitalized prisoners. Now this is the South Bronx we're talking about here. Nine times out of ten there are Perps in the hospital. More injured than sick, I might add. To make matters worse, the hospital is Lincoln Hospital. This hospital has the proud distinction of being rated the worse hospital in the city. Not just in the Bronx, but in the entire city! Just to give you an idea of how a hospital can achieve this status, a patient died in the waiting room and sat there dead for six hours until someone noticed. If that doesn't convince you then let me tell you about the poor fifteen year old boy that was shot in the head and robbed of his leather jacket. What's extra sad about this is that he wasn't a street wandering punk. The robbers went through his knapsack and when we arrived at the scene there were school books and a bible in the street. This kid was one of the few good ones living among these animals.

Anyway, the poor kid is lying there, still alive with a bullet in his head. We rush him over to Lincoln Hospital hoping that there is a miracle waiting for this kid at the E.R. We should have taken him to Dr. Seuss. He would have had a better chance. I remember standing in the E.R.

watching the doctors work on him. The nurse is attempting to insert something in his inner thigh when I hear her say "Oops" as streams of blood start shooting across the room from the artery she just punctured. Now I know that he was a goner anyway, but that's just ridiculous. Upon seeing this, I turn to my partner and say "Dave, if I'm ever shot, please do not bring me here".

Anyway, now that I've proved my point, let me get back to guarding the Perps. There would be nights that I was so tired I would ask to go to Lincoln just so I could get some sleep! This can be dangerous, even life threatening. Hospitalized prisoners do try to escape, and they will stop at nothing to succeed. One of the scariest of these incidents happened to a cop in my command about ten years ago. Officer Don had about five years on at the time. The prisoner he was guarding asked him if he could use the bathroom. P.O. Don undid the handcuffs, prisoners are always handcuffed to the hospital bed and escorted him to the bathroom in the hall. P.O. Don waited patiently in the hallway unaware that the Perp is in the bathroom prying the metal bar from the wall that is there to help people in wheelchairs pull themselves onto the bowl.

All of a sudden, the Perp comes out swinging and is beating P.O. Don with the bar. Now he's fighting for his life. None of the doctors or nurses came to help Don. The Perp is beating Don and trying to grab Don's gun at the same time. Luckily, Don draws his gun and shoots and kills the bastard. Don is a bloody mess and lucky to be alive.

When you hear stories like this, you always pray that something like this never happens to you. My prayers were answered for my first four years on the job. Until, one night my partner and I are called in off patrol to go guard a hospitalized prisoner while the arresting officer finishes the paper work. I asked why doesn't her partner guard him? I was told that her partner went home sick. Dave and I were off to Lincoln. We really didn't mind. It was already five in the morning, there is only a few hours left. What could possibly happen? We didn't know it at the time, but it was going to get pretty exciting.

The Perp that we had to guard was a hulking 6'5", 260lb. monster who is drunk off his ass. Earlier in the night, this "gentleman" decided to break in and rob an apartment. But, the owner came home and beat his drunk ass breaking the Perps nose in the process. So here we are sitting in the E.R. with a bloody, drunken mess. We have one of his arms handcuffed to the bed that he's laying in. The only problem is that he insists on trying to get up. So I cuff his other arm to the bed so now he's lying there with both arms stretched out. "If you behave, I'll take off one of the cuffs." Sounds reasonable enough. But, the answer I get is "Fuck you," so I sit back down and continue reading my newspaper.

Now it's about six A.M. and the Perp is still struggling trying to get up, when all of a sudden he stops. I look up at him and see that he's staring at me. All of a sudden he spits on me. This big blood filled saliva glob. He scores a direct hit. I can instantly feel my rage meter go off the charts. This guy could have A.I.D.S. for all I know. I stand up and roll my newspaper up and smack him in the face with it. It's a good thing that I left my nightstick in the car because I would have killed the son of a bitch. I could see the headlines now. "White cop hits black prisoner with his nightstick while prisoner has both arms in cuffs. Al Sharpton would have had a field day with this. So I used my newspaper like I said. I smacked him with it and the animal pulls on the cuffs to raise one of his tree trunk legs and kick me in the chest knocking me back into the wall. As I regain my balance I see the monster is coming towards me dragging the bed! I pull out my mace, gave it a few shakes, aimed it point blank at his ugly mug and let him have it as I yelled, "Fuck you!" I shot that mace in his eyes, up his nose and in his mouth. I emptied the entire can as his screams filled the E.R. "Water!" "I need water! You win, get me some water!" " I always win," I said. Both of his arms are still in cuffs, so he can't rub his eyes. The best he can do is rub his face along the walls. I'm in such an intense frame of mind that I'm still looking for something to hit this guy with when my common sense kicks in and I tell myself enough, I got him.

All this happened in a matter of seconds that my partner didn't have time to react. The problem now is that the mace is so strong that all the hospital personal and the other patients are feeling the effects of the mace.

Everyone is coughing, and choking. I would hear the sound of the elevator doors opening immediately followed by coughing. One nurse comes up to me holding a mask on her face with tears in her eyes and she starts yelling at me. "Why did you do that? This is not the precinct, you can't do that here!" I said, "Listen, if he keeps it up, I'm gonna mace him again, so keep your mask on and be ready". Now the hospital staff has to move everyone to the other wing of the E.R. They start setting up big fans to help clear the air. I get on the phone and call the desk sergeant to inform him of the incident. He tells me he will notify the patrol sergeant to swing by. In the mean time, King Kong has finally settled down as the doctors try to treat his eyes, which are practically swollen shut. The doctor turns to me and says in a somewhat demanding tone, "I need you to take the cuffs off." I shake my head and say, "I'm not taking those cuffs off." "But I can't get him close enough to the sink to rinse his eyes," he explained. I shrug my shoulders and say, "I don't care, let them burn. Those cuffs don't come off until my sergeant shows up."

When my Sarge arrives, I explain what happened and he asked me if my chest hurts from being kicked. It didn't really hurt, but I told him it did because this was a golden opportunity to get some time off with a line of duty injury.

When I finally arrive back at the station house, I'm greeted by the arresting officer, P.O. Joann, who feels terrible that this happened. I told her not to worry about it, shit happens. It's not her fault.

I ended up getting two days off due to my "injury," and when I returned to work, I'm greeted by P.O. Joann with a homemade cake with my name on it. "I still feel terrible, I hope this helps," she said. I smiled, and gave her a hug and said, "Thanks, you didn't have to do this."

Let me tell you that the cake was delicious. It was so good that it was almost worth the trouble. Almost.

***

There was one other cop in my squad that had graduated the year before me and still didn't have a steady partner to work with. One night, while we were in the locker room changing into our uniforms, I approached Dave and asked him if he wanted to try being partners. He answered yes without hesitation. We let our sergeant know that we wanted to be partners and the next night we were on patrol together.

The first few nights working together, Dave and I would tell one another all about ourselves. Dave is married, has a beautiful young daughter and lives in Queens, not too far from my parents house. A couple of years later he would be blessed with a baby boy.

The fact that he only has a year more experience than I do made working together that much easier. I've heard plenty of rookies complain when working with seasoned veterans that they are told to just sit there and don't do anything. One rookie told me that the cop he was working with said to him on the first night, "Listen kid, I've got more time on this job than you do going to the bathroom. So I'll handle everything. Just sit there and learn." Some of these cops forget that they were once rookies too.

I didn't have this problem with Dave because he was still learning the job and we would look to each other for advice when handling jobs.

Our partnership would end up working out great. When it came to doing police work, Dave was just as uninterested in it as I was. All Dave wanted to do was finish the night and go home to his family. Don't get me wrong. We did our job properly, but we didn't make mountains out of mole hills. We would do what was necessary to complete the job.

When it came to making an arrest, both of us wanted no part of it. We both had no desire for the overtime nor did we want to go to court for the arrest down the road. But, sometimes we were left with no choice and had to arrest somebody. Dave and I would take turns making arrests. If he made the last arrest, even if it was six months ago, the next arrest would be mine. Of course if I had plans for the morning when it's my turn to take an arrest, then Dave would take it. I would do the same for Dave. But, if the situation called for an arrest, Dave and I would try to see if we could handle it without making the arrest.

One instance that stands out in my mind is the time we responded to a domestic dispute and when we arrived we were greeted at the door by a woman with a bloody nose. Her face was red and her eyes were full of tears. My baby's father hit me," she said. I realized during my training months that there are no husbands and wives in the South Bronx. It's either my baby's father or my baby's mother. Anyway, we asked her where he was and she pointed to the bedroom. Now this is an assault. It's a must arrest situation. I tried to open the bedroom door but it was locked from the inside. I could hear the television and instructed him to open the door. Of course he wasn't going to open the door, so I asked Dave what he suggested we do. " Well, I have to take my daughter to school in the morning" Dave said. Earlier in the night, I told Dave that I had a doctor's appointment in the morning so I couldn't take an arrest. This is a tough situation for us. When we asked the woman what she

97

wanted us to do, she replied with "I want him arrested!" My partner and I looked at each other and Dave said to the woman, "Look, he's locked himself in the bedroom. So just go to sleep in the other room and if he comes out, call 911 and we will come back and arrest him."

We both know that wasn't the right way to handle the situation. We should've kicked the door open and arrested him. But we both had shit to do in the morning. As far as we were concerned our personal lives take precedent over the job. If he opens the bedroom door, he's arrested. But he didn't and we were not going in after him.

One of the strangest and eeriest encounters that Dave and I experienced happened about two years ago and both of us still have no explanation for it.

One night while we were driving around on patrol, a woman pulls next to us and asks us if we can help her. "Officers, my neighbor across the street is playing his music so loud that me and my kids can't fall asleep." My partner and I follow her to her building and the music is so loud that we can hear it down the block. When we pull up to the building, I can see a huge speaker on the fifth floor fire escape and the music is unbearably loud. But, the thing that struck me as odd was that the music that was playing was rock and roll. This neighborhood is almost a complete Spanish speaking area. The only music that is played is Spanish music. When I heard the rock music playing I instantly became suspicious.

Dave and I start to walk upstairs, and when we reach the fourth floor, a guy comes out of his apartment and informs us about the guy who lives in the apartment on the fifth floor. "The guy that lives upstairs is really strange," he says. He then tells us that there are two doors in the hallway and that both doors lead to that apartment. We thank him for the info and continue on.

When Dave and I reach the fifth floor landing, we see the two doors that the guy told us about, but what's stranger about this is that both doors are missing their doorknobs and there is a big chain going through the doorknob holes and through the wall with a big padlock locking the doors shut.

The music is still blasting as I try to peek through one of the empty doorknob holes to see what's going on in there. But it's pitch black in the apartment and Dave and I both left our flashlights in the car. Since there was no way we were going to walk back down five flights to get our flashlights, we had to make do without them.

I didn't think that whoever is inside is going to hear me over the music if I knock on the door with my fist, so I take my police radio and use it to pound on the door several times as Dave tries to listen for a response. What we heard was a sound that neither one of us ever heard before and will never hear again. The only way I can describe it is that it sounded like a sick cat was being slowly tortured to death, combined with an asthmatic inhale. Whatever it was, it appeared that the loud music was being used as a cover.

I looked at Dave and said, "What the fuck was that?" Dave looked at me with eyes as wide as saucers and uttered, "I don't know." I pounded on the door several more times and we heard the noise again. I take a step back, draw my gun, and ask, "What are we doing?

We going in?" As I prepare to kick the door open, Dave looks at me, pauses for a moment and very quickly said, "No." I instantly holster my gun and we got the hell out of there.

During the rest of the night, we tried to come up with ideas on what made that noise. "I have no idea what that was, but whatever it was, it would've got sixteen rounds put into it", I said. Dave and I tried to tell the other cops about it but there was no way we could even come close to imitating the sound we heard.

For the rest of our time working together, we never had another complaint involving that apartment again. When I told my sister and her husband about it, they laughed and my brother-in-law says, "A story like that can only happen in the South Bronx at two in the morning."

When Dave and I reflect on that night, we are glad that we didn't have our flashlights with us. Who knows what the hell we would've seen in that apartment that night. We definitely believe that we were better off not knowing. After all, it is said that curiosity killed the cat, and that's good enough for me.

CHAPTER 18

The more pressure that the department puts on the cops to produce, the more disgruntled the cops become. If only the department would let cops be cops and do their jobs, situations like the one I just wrote about wouldn't happen. My first year on the job I didn't mind making arrests. I would write my fair share of summonses and would actually like going to work. But as time wore on, I realized that all the good work you do means nothing. You are only as good as your last months activity. If you were a good numbers guy every month, meaning you constantly had high summons numbers and made a good number of arrests, that is all forgotten if the following month you slaked off a little. What usually happens is your supervisor will tell you that your numbers are too low and the Captain isn't happy. The fact that your last six months activity was great is immaterial. As far as the

103

department is concerned, it's what have you done for me lately? Punishment for low activity can be a change of tours, or a foot post in the middle of nowhere. The problem is that most cops will continue to give low numbers just on spite. It' s a no win situation. But my hatred for the job was a combination of asshole supervisors and the politics involved with the department. What people don't realize is that the stress that cops deal with comes from within the department, not form the streets. Cops get more respect from civilians than they do from their supervisors.

One night at roll call, my partner and I are assigned to a 4:00 mealtime. But after roll call the desk sergeant changed our meal to 4:30. No big deal. It didn't matter to us. We grabbed our radios, got the car keys and went out on patrol.

Throughout the night we answered several jobs without any incidents. One call that we received was a call for drug sales at a specific location. When we pulled up to the location, we saw a man that fit the description. We walked up to him and asked him a few questions, did a quick frisk and found nothing. As a courtesy, my partner and I would always give the person a quick explanation on why we were "picking" on them before we left. Whenever a cop searches someone, the cop is required to fill out a stop, question and frisk form, which is called a UF250 in police jargon. My partner and I filled these out only on occasion, chalk it up to laziness. But, tonight my partner said, "We might as well do a 250". "O.K.," I said, and I proceeded to complete the small form. Filling out this 250 would end up being a blessing in disguise for us later on in the night.

Now the time is about 4:15 A.M. and my partner parked the patrol car on a nice quiet street so we can bullshit with each other as we waited for our mealtime. All of a sudden we are called into the command and as we pull up to the station house, we are met by our Sergeant who asks us what time our meal is. "Our meal is at 4:30, Sarge, "I replied." " Are you sure it wasn't 4:00," he asks. "We were assigned a 4:00 meal at roll call but the desk officer changed it to 4:30. Why? What's up? "Well, the captain was driving around and he saw you guys parked somewhere." "He thinks your meal is at 4:00 and that you are trying to take a later meal on purpose." After the Sarge finished, I showed him my memo book to show him that I documented the meal change. "Hey, I believe you guys" the Sarge said. "I just wanted to give you a heads up so you don't walk in and get ambushed by the captain." We thanked the Sarge and proceeded to walk into the house to get this over with.

As we walked through the doors, we see the captain standing there looking as unhappy as someone possibly could. Standing there with him is the Integrity control Lieutenant and the Desk Sergeant. Our sergeant would come in and join us a few seconds later. As soon as we walk up to them the captain starts screaming at us. "Officers! What time is your meal?" "Uh, 4:30, sir" I replied very calmly, "4:30!" "Not 4:00?" he screamed. "Um, no sir. It was 4:00 but the desk officer changed it to 4:30". I'm answering him in a voice as soft as possible hoping that it will make the Captain realize just how stupid he sounds screaming like an idiot. After he heard my answer, the Captain started to scream at the desk officer. "How the fuck am I supposed to know that they have a 4:30 meal if you don't change it on the roll call?" The desk officer can only stare at him with her mouth open, as the Captain grew redder with rage. My partner and I figured that we are in the clear. After all, we didn't do anything wrong. But the Captain isn't satisfied with that. Instead of either giving my partner and I a simple apology or at least telling us that we weren't at fault, the S.O.B. is going to get us on something. After the Captain was finished screaming at the Sergeants, even our Sergeant was screamed at, he turned his attention toward us. "Officer, how many summonses do you have for the month?" His question is directed at me. "Twenty five, sir." I could tell that my answer surprised him a little. He looks at my partner and asks, "what about you?" My partner pulls a summons out of his memo book and says, "with this one, twenty three." It just so happens that last month our summons count was not that good and our Sergeant kindly asked us if we could pick it up. So this month my partner and I gave out a little more summonses than usual to make up for it.

After the Captain found that he couldn't get us for a low summons count, he tried something else. "I bet you haven't written any 250's tonight," he said to me with sarcasm in his voice and a look on his face to go with it that it still pisses me off to this day when I think about it.

After hearing his snotty accusation, I couldn't help but smile at him as I said, "Actually sir, I did do a 250 tonight." I could see the Captains lips curl up with frustration. Now the Captain has to resort to flat out lying to make my partner and I look as if we are guilty of something. "Well, I saw you guys parked and I drove through the stop sign twice and you didn't do anything about it." First of all, where we were parked there was no stop sign. Besides, we know which unmarked car the Captain drives, so if he did blow a stop sign, we wouldn't do anything because we know it's him. But my partner and I remained silent as the Captain continued. "Not only that, but there was a Perp standing right behind your patrol car smoking a joint and you officers failed to take police action!" I felt like asking the Captain if I had the word "stupid" tattooed on my fore head. If anyone had the balls to smoke a joint behind a police car with two cops sitting in it, I would love to meet them. Also, if the Captain saw this then why didn't he alert us to the situation, even for our own safety? I'll tell you why, because the Captain isn't man enough to admit he is wrong. Instead of being glad that two of his officers weren't trying to get over with a later meal and were actually out there giving him good summons numbers, the asshole was pissed that he couldn't nail us on something. My partner and I looked at each other and rolled our eyes. The Captain turned his attention back toward the Sergeant when he suddenly looked at us and said, "You two are clueless!" My partner and I stood there dumbfounded. Before the Captain could continue, our Sergeant jumped in and asked, "Sir, can they go to meal?" "Yeah, go to meal," he said in disgust as he shooed us away with his hand.

Now the time is 5:30. This whole fiasco lasted over an hour. The Captain was pissed because he thought we were trying to take an unauthorized later meal and we end up getting a 5:30 meal thanks to the Captain. My partner and I could only laugh as we spoke about it with each other later on.

I think that it was from this moment on that I started to get fed up with the department and started to care less and less about it. Why should I care about a job that only looks to fuck me any chance it gets? Would you?

CHAPTER 19

As time wore on, I found that I was changing. My personality was being affected by the job. People in any profession that deal with the pain and suffering of others, such as cops, firemen, doctors, etc., usually become "cold" after a while and won't show any emotion when they see people hurt or in need of help. But I was changing in another way that I didn't like. Every night, when it was getting close to the time for me to get ready to leave for work, my whole demeanor would change. I became impatient and even worse, I became short tempered towards my wife. I was like a Jekyll and Hyde. I would travel the entire twenty minutes to work in a bad mood. I actually started to hate going to work. Once I was at work, I wouldn't start feeling better until I was on patrol with my partner and we tell each other how much we hate doing this. What would make matters worse would be when we would get involved in something that would make me even more disgusted with the job.

It could be something stupid like Captain jackass screaming at us for something we didn't do, or it could be something minor like the time we came out of a housing project to find our patrol car covered in saliva. The windows, the door handles, everything was spit upon. It was disgusting. What the satisfaction could be to spit on a police car eludes me, but I guess that's all part of being a cop. As time went on and my morale lessened and my hatred for the job grew, it would be only a matter of time before I get jammed up. Since I was caring less and less about the job, I started to give almost no activity and I started to talk back to supervisors.

In the last few months that I remained on the job, there were several instances that occurred that would combine to push me passed the point of no return.

The first happened in the month of March. As me and the rest of the midnight crew were waiting for roll call, the Sergeant informed us that an Inspector was going to turn us out at roll call so we should make sure that we have all of our equipment and that our shoes are shined and our uniforms look halfway decent.

This particular Inspector, who I will name Inspector Moron, was known to be a real hard ass who wouldn't hesitate to give a cop a C.D. for whatever he could. The rank of Inspector is the next rank after Captain, and the rank just below Chief. This rank is very powerful within the department. If an Inspector wants to screw a cop, all it would take is one phone call to your commanding officer and the next day you will be transferred to wherever, doing whatever that Inspector wants you to do.

Inspector Moron had stood in on a midnight roll call a week prior to this one and luckily it was my squads' regular day off. We were told that he didn't like the way one of the midnight Sergeants conducted the roll call and proceeded to scream at him in front of the cops and the very next day that Sergeant was transferred to the day tour. So now Inspector Moron is back and this time it's our turn to deal with him.

During roll call, we are given assignments for the night and are informed of any problem areas that we should be aware of. At the end of roll call, we are then instructed to prepare for inspection. The Sergeant and the Inspector walk back and forth, examining each cop for things like a clean uniform, a working flashlight and a neat appearance.

One by one, each cop was criticized by the Inspector for any little thing he could find. As I stood at attention waiting for Inspector Moron to reach me, I gave myself a quick look over and thought that I looked pretty acceptable. My shoes were shinny, my flashlight had fresh batteries and I was cleanly shaven. But the one thing that I didn't notice was the condition of my turtleneck. During the winter, we could either wear the typical blue uniform shirt or an N.Y.P.D. turtleneck under our jacket. I always went with the turtleneck because it is so much more comfortable than the uniform shirt. But after a while of continuous use, the neck of the shirt becomes stretched and will start to sag instead of staying close around the throat. As I stand there unaware of this, Inspector Moron steps up to me, looks at me up and down, points to my turtleneck and asks "Officer, what's with the pajamas?" I didn't know how to respond to that or if I even should respond so I just stood there. Inspector Morons' next question was "Officer, how much time do you have on the job?" "Almost five years," I said with a small grin. "Well, don't you think it's about time you washed that jacket?" he snapped. "Yes sir" I said in a low, dejected tone. As the Inspector took a step towards Freddy, who was the officer standing to my right, he turned and looked back at me and added, "You know you look like a disgrace" to which I gave no response. As the Inspector started to focus his attention back towards Fred, he looked at him, and in one motion stood in front of Fred and yelled out "Jesus Christ, I hit the jackpot!" As I fought to hold in my laughter, I glanced over at Fred to see what the Inspector was referring to. The one aspect that stood out was Fred's' big beer belly that his bulletproof vest couldn't fit over. I looked as if Fred was wearing a bib instead of his vest.

Also, Fred was missing his cap device. The cap device is a type of badge that is affixed to the front of our police hat. And last but not least, his turtleneck was just as worn out as mine. "Officer, where is your cap device?" Before Fred could react, the Inspector continued. "And look at your uniform, it's a mess!" Inspector Moron then pointed to me and said, "I want to see you two after roll call!"

When the Inspector dismissed us, he called Fred and I over to him. "Officers, when you put this uniform on you represent the Police Department. If I was a victim and you two showed up I would think that I'm dealing with a couple of bums!" Fred and I would just nod as the Inspector ranted on. Inspector looked at Fred and asked him where his cap device was. "I lost my hat and bought a new one. I ordered a new cap device but it takes about ten days to get it" Fred explained. That was true but it wasn't good enough for the Inspector. "Do you have the receipt," the Inspector asked. Fred shrugged his shoulders and said, "I might have it in my locker." "Well go get it," the Inspector demanded. "And you, your dismissed!" he told me.

I didn't have a problem with this moron reprimanding me about my uniform. But what bothered me was the fact

115

that the Inspector was wearing green rubber winter boots, that are not authorized by the Department to wear in uniform. So, before this asshole criticizes us on our uniforms, he should be wearing the proper uniform from head to toe. I'm not going to listen to a hypocrite.

There was one question that I was dying to ask Inspector Moron but I chose not to. I wanted to ask him, "If you're an Inspector making six figures a year, why are you coming to the South Bronx during the midnight shift to bust our balls? Wouldn't you rather be at home in bed with your wife?"

I just don't get it. It's not like the Mayor is going to call this guy at home to tell him what a good job he's doing keeping us in line. Sometimes I think that supervisors like this one go home and tell their families at the dinner table how they let a couple of cops have it. All I was thinking during his "assault" on me was that I'm one of the good guys. The mug shots on the wall are the bad guys. I get more respect from them than I do from the department I work for.

I would think that the higher in rank you go, the happier you would be. But, the problem is that if someone is an asshole as a cop, as they move up in rank, they become bigger assholes. Every time I think that I encountered the biggest asshole on this job, someone comes along to prove me wrong.

CHAPTER 20

There was this one particular Lieutenant that claimed the "biggest asshole" title. Since I retired before I could meet another serious "contender," the Lieutenant will hold this title forever.

I only worked with this Lieutenant for my last remaining months, but in that short time I realized that with pricks like this guy, the department is really going down the drain.

When Lieutenant Prick first arrived to my command, he was assigned to the midnight tour. At first, he seemed like an okay guy. He was soft spoken and took time to explain what he expected from us on a daily basis. But, as the next few weeks passed, I came to realize that he was nothing but a back stabbing son of a bitch that looked to jam cops up.

My downfall with Lieutenant Prick all started one night when my partner and I were called into the precinct off patrol. As we were driving towards the precinct, I said to my partner "the Lieutenant is going to make us transport prisoners." What this means is that when cops from the earlier tours make an arrest, their prisoner is kept in the precinct holding cells until the cop is done with the arrest paperwork. After the cop finishes the prisoner is then taken to central booking so they can see the judge in the morning. But, if the arresting officer is on overtime due to the arrest, the department rules do not allow the arresting officer to transport his own prisoner to C.B. while on overtime. This is so because sometimes you can be at C.B. for hours waiting to lodge in your prisoner, and the city doesn't want to pay all that overtime.

When the arresting officer needs his or her prisoner transported, a sector from the next tour will transport the prisoner for that particular officer. So, if it's a day tour cop with the arrest, then a 4 x 12 sector will transport. If it's a 4 x 12 cop, then the midnight will transport, and so on.

The problem that I have with this rule is that most of the arrests that we end up transporting are these bullshit trespassing arrests or minor drug arrests, like a homeless guy that was busted for carrying a crack pipe that had some residue on it like I had explained earlier. Most of these arrests are done by the plain clothes cops that need to make any arrest they can to either meet the necessary quota or they need the overtime. The joke about this is that when I look at the arrest paperwork, the time of arrest could be 9:00 p.m. for example, but it's now 4:00 in the morning and the cop is finnally finishing the arrest process. Since the plain clothes cops tour ends and 2:00 a.m., that's a couple of hours overtime for them and I get stuck transporting their Perps. I can process an arrest in as little as forty five minutes. These cops get away with dragging out their arrest process for hours to get the overtime, but they can't transport their own Perps. I really wouldn't mind so much, but the problem is that these cops work in teams of four to six cops and they arrest as many as six people at once. Now my partner and I are stuck transporting their mess. On top of that, the paperwork is usually wrong or incomplete and we have to sit in C.B. correcting their mistakes.

So, I say to my partner "The Lieutenant is going to make us transport prisoners." "Are you sure,?" Dave asks. "Yeah, I saw the street crime guys come in with five Perps."

But, this is bullshit because we have plenty of rookies on the midnights that can transport but the Lieutenant always calls us. After all, part of being a rookie is having to do things like transport Perps. I handled more than my share of shitty assignments during my first few years. I've also had Perps get to C.B. and complain that they are sick, so now I have to take them to the hospital and sit with them until a doctor sees them. As we pull up to the precinct I tell my partner that I don't want to transport these bullshit arrests. We walk in and Lieutenant Prick says, "Mike, I need you guys to transport five Perps." I immediately shake my head and say, "No, I'm not doing it. Give me the C.D. because I won't do it!" The Lieutenant looks at me a little confused and asks, "Mike, what's wrong?" "I always transport for these fucking guys and I'm not doing it!" My tone has increased at this point and I can see other cops that were hanging out look away in disbelief. I quickly calmed down and said, "It doesn't matter, I'll do it. I'm sorry." My partner and I grabbed the paperwork, escorted the Perps into the police van and drove off to C.B. Of course, I had to refinger print two of the Perps and correct some of the paperwork when we got there becasuue it was done half wrong.

The next night, Dave and I are finishing up our meal hour, and when we walk passed the desk, the Lieutenant says "Dave, Mike, don't go anywhere. I have six Perps for you to transport." The slight grin he expressed combined with the sarcastic tone in his voice nearly made me say something that I would've regretted. We transported the six pot smoking menaces of society and I knew that from now on this prick was going to fuck with me any chance he got. I felt bad for Dave because since he's my partner, he's going to suffer along with me.

CHAPTER 21

For the next several months, Dave and I would be given all the shitty assignments that came up. "Man, I can't wait for my five year anniversary so I can vest out." If I said that to my partner once, I said it a million times. My date of appointment was July 18, 1996. On July 18, 2001 I will be eligible to vest out. What that means is that I can retire and in fifteen years I will start collecting a pension and will receive my medical benefits and I had to tolerate Lieutenant Pricks' bullshit for only a few more months.

I didn't know how low this Lieutenant could go in trying to jam up a cop until one night a homeless women walks into the precinct to inform the Lieutenant that she witnessed a cop hitting his police car with a sledge hammer. The woman informs him of the number on the car and the Lieutenant calls that car into the command. When Chris pulls up, the Lieutenant sees that there are three small dents in the cars hood. In the trunk of the car there is a big sledge hammer. He asks Chris if he used the sledge hammer at any time during the night. Chris explained that earlier in the night he noticed an old refrigerator laying on the sidewalk that still had it's door attached to it. That can become a dangerous situation if any kids decide to play around with the fridge and become locked inside it.

The patrol guide states that if a discarded refrigerator is found with it's door still attached, then the officer will call for emergency service, (ESU), to come remove the door. But, since Chris knew that there was a sledge hammer in the trunk and he didn't want to bother ESU at three in the morning for something like this, he figured he and his partner would do it themselves.

What this homeless woman saw was Chris hitting the refrigerator and assumed that he was striking the patrol car. As for the three dents in the hood, those have been there for over a year. Besides, anyone with a little common sense could see that if Chris would've hit the car with that sledge hammer, the damage would've been much more extensive than three little dings in the hood.

Whose story do you think Lieutenant Prick believes? If you said the homeless woman, you're right. I'm not calling him Lieutenant Prick for nothing. The Lieutenant immediately calls Internal Affairs. He then calls our commanding officer at home to inform him about what Chris has "done." But, the Lieutenant doesn't stop there. He wants fingerprints taken from the sledge hammer, the car, and the refrigerator. He wants a crime scene set up so nobody will touch the police car or the fridge. And last but not least, he wants to have Chris treated as an E.D.P. (Emotionally disturbed person)!

The Lieutenant is hell bent on fucking Chris and it's all based on a homeless womans' assumption. I guess the Lieutenant never took into consideration what drugs she might be on or how much alcohol she has drank. If she says she saw it, then it must be true. The fact that Chris' partner has stated in a written statement that Chris did not at any time hit the police car with the hammer means nothing. Lieutenant Prick will take the word of a cracked out homeless person over a cops any day.

Now the Lieutenant is calling in all the other sectors so he can examine their cars. I guess he figures that if one cop is going to smash a police car with a hammer, then we all are.

Lieutenant Prick really has the ball rolling now. There are inspectors, and chiefs walking in and out of the command involved in this investigation. But, the best part of this mess that he started comes at 8:00 in the morning when the fleet manager arrives. The fleet manager is the cop that is assigned to maintain the cars. He keeps track of things like the mileage so the cars can be sent for oil changes at the proper times. He also keeps a log indicating any new damage done to the cars along with the date of occurrence. When the fleet manager shows up for work that morning, he is informed on what has transpired and he immediately gets the file on the car Chris was using that night, and walks up to Lieutenant Prick and says, "Hey, Lieutenant. I documented these dents in the hood of that car over a year ago." Now what is the prick going to do. He started this whole cluster fuck and Chris is innocent. The investigation is closed out as unfounded. But, the Lieutenant can't accept the fact that Chris was innocent, when he was so sure he was guilty. Just for good measure, the Lieutenant has Chris kicked off the midnights and put on the day tour. What a guy.

CHAPTER 22

July 18th can't come fast enough. What ever morale was left on the midnights has been sucked dry by this Lieutenant. Both the cops and the Sergeants can't stand him. Lieutenant Prick wants more and more numbers. Instead of four arrests a year, he now wants one a month. He wants road blocks done every night to boost the summons count. The more he squeezed us, the more bitter the cops became. I stopped writing summonses all together. I'm done in a few mnths so I could care less about his numbers.

One night, May 6th to be exact, I was assigned to the hospital to guard a prisoner. As I was walking upstairs to the locker room to get a book to take with me, I see my friend Ed walking downstairs towards me. We both stop on the steps to talk to each other, and as I turn towards

Ed, I slip off the step and fall backwards. I put my hand out to stop my fall, and I end up jamming my hand into the step breaking the top knuckle on my right ring finger. "Mike, are you all right?" Ed asked with a slight giggle. "I thnk I just broke my finger," I said as I showed him that my finger tip is facing west instead of north.

I walk back downstairs and show my Sergeant my finger and it totally grossed her out. She told me to call an ambulance and go to the hospital. "While you're at the hospital, I'll start the line of duty injury paperwork,", she said. She then asked, "were there any witnesses?" "Yeah, I was talking to Eddie when it happened," I said. "Tell him to see me before he leaves," the Sarge said. "I need him to fill out a witness statement." I nodded and told Eddie. The ambulance came and I went to the hospital. The doctor looked at my x-rays and showed me where the break was and told me it will take about six weeks for it to heal. He opened up a splint, taped it up and sent me on my way. It didn't' really bother me. I've had worse injuries throughout my life.

I then had to go to the police surgeon to see how long I was going to be kept out of work. Before I walked into his office I taped my broken finger to my middle finger just to make it look worse than it was.

After all was said and done, I was out of work for two months. The police surgeon didn't put me back until July 8th. Those two months that I was off was just what I needed. I didn't miss the job at all. At one point my father asked me if I missed the job. "What job?" I asked. "Point taken," he said.

In the middle of my "vacation" my friend Bruce calls me to see how I'm feeling. He then says "Mike, did you know that you're not on the midnights anymore?" "Bruce, I haven't been to work in a month. No one told me anything" I said in a shocked tone. Bruce works upstairs in the administrative office and went on to explain that he received a phone call from the C.O. telling Bruce to leave a note for the administrative Lieutenant that he wants officer DeMarino off midnights. Bruce said he could hear Lieutenant Prick in the background giving the C.O. my name. The s.o.b. waited for me to be out so I couldn't fight it. So now I have to finish my time on the 4 x 12 tour.

Breaking my finger was the best thing that could have happened to me. I went back to work with only eight days left to reach my retirement date. What was even better was that the police surgeon didn't put me back to full duty. I was returned on limited duty status. That means I have to be kept off patrol until I am reexamined by the police surgeon and he determines that I am capable of full duty. So, for the time being, I will be inside answering the phones.

CHAPTER 23

My big day has arrived. I head down to police headquarters and complete the paperwork necessary to vest out. The young lady tells me that I have to give the city a thirty day notice so my official retirement date is August 16. I should be on limited duty status right into my retirement. Just knowing that I have a month left has lifted a weight off my shoulders and I feel like a new man.

When I tell my wife the news, she is even happier than I am. "Now we can lead a normal life," she said. She then said something that made me feel awful. "You were becoming a real prick at times." After hearing that, I hugged her and apologized. This job had gotten the best of me. It had a submission hold on me and I tapped out, I threw in the towel. It's a shame because it really can be a great job. I had a lot of good times with my partner and the other cops I've worked with. But, it's beyond the point of no return. With the growing pressure put on cops to perform along with the lack of respect cops get from within the department is tearing this job apart. You read more and more about cops jumping ship to join other city agencies or choose other career paths. When I would talk to my father about the job, I would tell him how most of the cops are fed up or just hate the job altogether. My father would look at me like I was crazy and would tell me that he loved the job back when he was a cop. My response to that would be that this isn't the sixties anymore. The job is different now. 'How different could it be?" He would ask.. I would get frustrated trying to convince him of this, when one day while we were fisning on the Long Island Sound, the N.Y.P.D. Harbor Patrol pulled up to our boat to do an inspection. When I showed my police I.D. to the cop, we started to bullshit about the job. 'How much time do you have left?" My father asked. "Man, I got eight years left and I can't fucking wait. It can't come soon enough". My father shook his head and said 'That bad, huh?" "It sucks" Was his reply. Harbor Patrol was one of the most coveted details within the department. You either need a serious hook or would have to catch Jack the Ripper to earn the right to request a transfer to Harbor Patrol. Hearing his answers to my old man's questions brought a smile to my face. After a few more minutes of conversation, the police boat drove off and my father said "I can't believe that this guy wants to quit with the detail he's in, and to top it off he tells me the job sucks". I looked at my dad and said "I told you, it's not just me".

A few months ago, the NYPD visited a U.S. Marines base to promote the job and hopefully get applicants. Out of the fifty thousand marines stationed there, only twenty five signed up for the exam. People aren't stupid. No matter what the department says or does to make this job look attractive, the bottom line is money. The salary that cops earn in comparison to what is expected of them is so out of whack that the citizens of this city are lucky that cops do anything at all. I feel that I escaped this job at the right time. The department is getting more and more desperate for applicants. It's lowering it's standards and making it even easier to become a cop. Don't be surprised if in the next five to seven years there is a rise in police misconduct and police brutality. The cops that are being hired are only a step up from the Perps that they are arresting. The fact that N.Y.C. is the safest large city in America isn't going to last for long so enjoy it while it lasts, but at the same time don't be shocked when crime starts to soar. The department is filled with unhappy cops. It's only going to continue to get worse. My heart goes out to all of them.

CHAPTER 24

August 16 has come and gone. I said my goodbyes and closed that chapter of my life. I am a civilian once again. Sometimes I regret taking the job because I wonder what I would've done with my life in those five years instead of being a cop. When Raquel and I drove to my parents house to tell them the news, my mother hugged me and said, "As long as you're happy, that's the important thing." As my father shook my hand he said, "Well, you made a decision and you stuck to it. I wish you luck." But, he then asked me, "What are you going to do now?" I chuckled to myself, looked at my father and said, "Dad, I would shovel shit and collect cans instead of being a New York City Police Officer.

An Afterthought

As I reflect on my experience as a member of the N.Y.P.D., I can't help but have mixed feelings about it. Even though this will sound contradicting, those five years on the job were some of the worst times in my life, but were also some of the best. I wonder what path my life would have taken if I never accepted the job. But, I don't think it does any good to look back at what might have been. You must always look forward and do your best. The N.Y.P.D. gave me an opportunity to see how the "other" part of society lives. The part that is ruled by drugs, violence and poverty. Growing up, I would see ghettos and slums on TV. or I would occasionally drive by them on my way to somewhere, but I never set foot in them. I never knew what life was like for the people living there. Becoming a cop opened up that world to me. I saw the struggles of the hard working people trying to just survive each day and maybe make a better life for their families to then dealing with the dregs of society who don't care about their neighbors or the neighborhood they live in. As long as they get what they want either by stealing, selling drugs or killing. It's a shame that more times than not, the neighborhood gives into these animals and the areas appearance reflects the crime that it inhabits. Think of it like this. When neighborhoods are built, and new apartment buildings are constructed, the planners and construction workers didn't draw blue prints of slums. Someone didn't say "Hey, lets build a slum here." What they build are new buildings for people to rent and live. But, it's the people that turn the areas into slums.

It's the people that litter, deface property, bring drugs into the mix, and just don't care. Every time I would enter an apartment to handle a problem, I would end up either disgusted or just grossed out at the living conditions these people dwell in. There would be cat-sized rats, giant cockroaches, rotting food all over, crap on the walls and garbage everywhere. I even saw a dead cat in the corner of one apartment. How do you live with a dead cat? The sad part is when a little child walks out of a room to see you. How can you raise a child like this? It boggles my mind. The problem is that a lot of these people are either uneducated, drug addicts, or just plain lazy. They don't want to work. They live off of welfare, food stamps and other types of government aid. Most of them are from other countries where they probably lived like slobs also, but here in America you have the freedom and the right to live like a slob and the government will support you. If someone is content with this life style, then where is the incentive to change? This isn't living, it's surviving. There is no purpose to their lives. The only reason why they wake up in the morning is that they didn't die in their sleep. I can honestly say that my time on the job has given me a new found respect and an overall gratefulness of how fortunate I am to have the life I have. It's very easy to take things for granted, or to be jealous of what the other guy has, when you should realize you have more than most. I also feel that the job made me a stronger person mentally, and made me realize that I'm pretty good at handling life threatening situations that require split second decisions.

I only mentioned a fraction of a percent of what I encountered in my five years. There were mornings I would come home and my wife would ask me how my night was. "Kind of boring", I would tell her. But, as I would take my clothes off to take a shower, she would ask, "then how did you get those bruises on your arm?"

"Don't worry about it" I would say. "It's no big deal". I don't want to tell her that I got attacked by a Perp I was fingerprinting and I had to literally break his shoulder to stop him. She didn't' need to worry anymore than she did every time I left to go to the Bronx to start my tour.

The city is a big and dangerous place that puts it's cops to the test every minute of the day. I hope this book will help you understand a little of what cops face, from both the streets and the department itself. Next time you encounter a cop that might be short tempered or impatient with you, try to remember that the cop is a person, not a drone with no feelings or emotion. It's quite possible that the cop is having a bad day at work, just like we all experience from time to time and you need to cut him or her some slack.

When it's all said and done and I'm alone with my thoughts, I try to think about the good times I had with the job. I think about my partner, and I'm thankful that we still stay in touch. I think of the friends I made on the job and wish the m all the very best. I miss the job, but I don't miss the department. I remember an old timer that was in my precinct the last two years of his thirty five year career. He became a cop in the early sixties. That's four separate decades of witnessing change in the department.

I'm going to steal a quote that he once said to me when I asked him how the job was back in the sixties and seventies. He said, and I quote "They took a great job and they fucked it up." Enough said.

Made in the USA
Middletown, DE
06 December 2021

54402532R00085